Love From the Depths

Also by TOMIHIRO HOSHINO

Kaze no Tabi —published by Rippu Shobo in 1982
(English Version "Journey of the Wind" in 1988)

Kagirinaku Yasashii Hanabana—published by Kaisei-sha Publishing Co.,Ltd
in 1986
(English Version "Here So Close, but I Didn't Know" in 1988

Suzu no Naru Michi—published by Kaisei-sha Publishing Co.,Ltd in1988
(English Version"Road of the Tinkling Bell" in 1990)

Giniro no Ashiato—published by Inochino Kotoba-sha in 1988
(English Version "Silver Footprints" in 1994)

Hayasa-no-chigau Tokei—published by Kaisei-sha Publishing Co., Ltd in 1992

All of the original works in Japanese became best-sellers

Love
From
the Depths

THE STORY OF TOMIHIRO HOSHINO

by TOMIHIRO HOSHINO

Translated by
Deborah Stuhr Iwabuchi
&
Kazuko Enda

RIPPU SHOBO
Tokyo

First English Translation published in 1994
by Rippu Shobo Company Tokyo, Japan

Original Japanese Version published in 1981
by Rippu Shobo Company

Inquiries should be addressed to Rippu Shobo Company
5-5-8 Kamimeguro, Meguro-ku, Tokyo 153, Japan

ISBN4-651-14014-9
Printed in Japan
by Tosho Insatsu Company

Book Designed by Sono Saito
Edited by Sonoko Yamazaki

I can only say to others
What is second-most important in my thoughts
I cannot say what I want to say the most

Maybe it is because of this frustration
That I draw pictures
And sing songs

Maybe I long for people
In the hope of
Telling them what I want to say the most

CONTENTS

My friend pushed my wheelchair outside
    under a cherry tree
And bent down a branch in full bloom
    burying my face in blossoms

Filled with irresistible joy
    I began
Munching on the flowers
    blooming closest to my mouth

(Cherry blossoms 1977)

[RIGHT]
Picture and poem by TOMIHIRO HOSHINO,
accomplished with a brush held in his mouth.

車椅子を押してもらって
桜の木の下まで行く
友人が枝を曲げると
私は満開の花の中に埋ってしまった
湧き上ってくる感動をおさえることができず
私は口の周りに咲いていた
桜の花をむしゃむしゃと
食べてしまった

CHAPTER ONE

The Sad Blue Sky

June 17 to 20, 1970

(Potato Blossom)

From the Doctor's Report —

Attending physician, Dr. Nishimura of
the orthopedic unit, Gunma University Hospital

The patient fell head down while demonstrating a flip during school club activities and received a severe blow to the cervical area. At the time of hospitalization, there was complete paralysis of all four limbs. Symptoms include: sensory disturbance beneath the upper end of the sternum, dull response, shallow breathing by means of abdominal respiration, fever, critical condition with danger of asphyxia and cardiac arrest, anuria (inability to urinate), urinary and bowel disturbance, low blood pressure, shock. Patient constantly complains of pain in the cervical area.

Treatment: Oxygen inhalation, vein incision

Diagnosis: Fracture-dislocation of the anterior part of the fourth cervical vertebra and cervical spinal cord injury

June 19th: Opened holes in skull in order to put patient in traction to extend the dislocated vertebra. Breathing is still shallow and painful.

June 20th: Nose bleeding due to the catheter inserted in nose for oxygen inhalation. As head is turned upward, blood flows down nose to trachea, clogging and causing breathing difficulty. Gauze packing is applied to nose, but respiratory complications continue.

My Sister's Reminiscences

When we arrived at the hospital, we were relieved to see him looking cheerful and alert. We could hardly believe it when the doctor in charge told us that he was in critical condition. They had taken X-rays and found his neck broken and were concerned that he might stop breathing at any moment. The doctor said that he was paralyzed from his shoulders down, and I realized this was true when I touched him and there was no response at all.

To see a respirator, intravenous feeding, blood transfusion apparatus, and all sorts of other tubes pushed into such a robust and healthy body was totally bewildering. Despite all that,

Tomihiro continued to pretend that he was fine; he kept talking away, trying to keep us from worrying. But when he asked me questions about his childhood, I did not know what to say. My feeling was one of panic and overwhelming sadness.

June 17, 1970

It had finally stopped raining and was as if the clouds had been washed away leaving a broad, blue sky. After my physical education classes were finished for the day, I went to the school caretaker's room and took out a big paper bag which I had stashed in a locker. The bag was full of dirty underwear. I had not done any laundry at all since April, when I had begun teaching at Kuragano Junior High School in Takasaki City; I had just kept stuffing it away in the bag. I noticed that there were even some moldy items left over from my senior year in college. The next day I was to go with the eighth graders on a three-day field trip to Lake Haruna, and I was determined to get my underwear collection taken care of before then.

The caretaker's room was no more than a dark little hut. Against one wall was a washing machine, and from the window next to it I could see the blue sky. It was such a transparent, deep blue that I felt deep emotions stir inside me.

How can I waste this beautiful afternoon doing laundry? I thought. The kids are practicing in the gym; I'll run around with them instead! With little regret I abandoned the paper bag on the spot and ran off.

After school the gym was filled with the ruckus of pounding feet and the shrill voices of the students marking time. There was always lots of excitement and energy.

The members of the gymnastics club were just finishing mat work and about to move on to the next exercise. They saw me as I entered the gym with a salute, and welcomed me with eager smiles. One look at them and I was sure I had made the right decision.

There are three events in Japanese junior-high gymnastics: floor exercise, exercise bar, and vaulting horse. The bar is dangerous, so the students were not allowed to use it without me there. Instead they were practicing jumps on the springboard for the vaulting horse. This springboard was the same as that used in the Olympics and had been introduced to junior-high gymnastics a few years before. Learning to effectively use the elasticity of the board is an important point in mastering the vaulting horse.

First I did warm-up exercises on the mat where the girls were working out. Then I lined up with the boys. With the new springboard, it was possible to jump more than two meters high. I loved that feeling of being suspended in mid-air. Standing in front of the board, I felt an excited thrill run through me. I went from a roll to a flip. When the students did it, they kept trying to jump and turn at the same time, preventing themselves from getting enough leverage. So, I deliberately broke the jump into three separate steps—take-off, jump and flip—to show them how to do it. To prevent injuries in case of a fall, we laid out a twenty-centimeter-thick foam-rubber pad on top of the regular mat. Once again I stood in front of the springboard. I took a few practice bounces, then, swinging my arms upwards, I jumped on the board and rose toward the ceiling. Next I rolled up into a ball and began to turn. It crossed my mind that this feeling of soaring through the air was just like being on a trampoline—*bam*! Suddenly there was a loud noise, and I found myself staring up at the gym ceiling. The intertwining steel framework seemed farther away than usual and was turning slowly. The basketball team was practicing in the other half of the gym, and the sound of dribbling resounded harshly in my ears.

What was that first sound I had heard? Had something fallen onto the roof? And how long, I wondered, was I going to continue lying there? The students must be waiting to take their turns. Had I got so lazy I could not even sit up?

I must have lain there absentmindedly for a while before I realized that the basketball dribbling had stopped and the energy-filled air of the gym was now full of murmurs. Students had started to crowd around me. What am I doing? I thought. I should have been on my feet by now. I hastily tried to get up; but nowhere in my body did that idea seem to catch on. In fact, it vanished instantly without leaving a trace. I struggled. Struggled, but there was no way to make my body move. I felt hot, and my arms and legs seemed to have lost their form and evaporated into thin air. An awful thought crossed my mind, and I decided to test it. I called Okada, a seventh grader, who was watching me anxiously.

"Would you hold up my hand?" Okada picked up something at my side, but I could not see it. "A little higher."

I recognized the object as my own plump arm. I could not, however, feel his fingers holding mine, nor did I have any sensation of my limb being raised. Loneliness as cold as ice flooded in on me. I wondered if I was going to be like this forever.

The gym clock said five forty-five.

"Hoshino-*sensei!* What happened!" Mrs. Tanaka, who taught girl's P.E., came running. Someone must have thought it strange that I had not moved and run to get her.

"I think something's happened to my neck." I tried to say offhandedly what I most feared. Among the noisy crowd of students around me I picked out the vice-principal and some of the other teachers. I was surprised and relieved to see that most of them were still at school.

Only two months had passed since I had become a teacher. Actually, I still felt like a student. Even when my pupils addressed me as *sensei,* I could not respond immediately. When I was with another teacher, I was careful not to reply until I was sure that I was the one being called. In front of more experienced teachers I often forgot that I was no longer a teenager in a student uniform. About a month before, during gymnastics practice, I had broken a springboard and thought, *Oh no!*

Am I in trouble now! I had had a clear mental picture of myself being soundly scolded and had smiled wryly to myself.

Seeing that I could not get up, Mrs. Tanaka, long experienced in gymnastics, probably guessed what had happened.

"Uchibori's good, I think." She murmured the name of a local orthopedic surgeon. It was decided that I should go right away, and, as no other means were available, someone brought the school's small pickup truck around to the gym. I was lifted—mat and all—and placed in the back of the truck. Students, faces full of concern, surrounded the mat as I was carried out of the gym. Their voices and conversations were jumbled together sounding to me like a tape on "fast forward." I heard one voice say, "He oughta just die!" Then the quick retort of Mrs. Tanaka, "Shut up!" I recalled a student I had struck in anger a few days before in class.

By the time I asked Mr. Igarashi, a science teacher, to call my eldest sister in Isesaki, it had become so difficult to breathe that I had to force out each word one at a time. Lying there in the truck in exactly the same position as I had fallen, I finally lost the energy to speak and became silent. I kept my eyes wide open, though. They were all I had to depend on, and I was afraid to close them. Mrs. Tanaka had taken off her warm-up jacket and laid it gently over me. I could not feel it at all, but the warmth of her gesture came through, and I realized that she, too, lived in the world of sport. I had often done the same thing for friends who had been injured in some sport or another, but I had never personally realized how comforting such a small action could be.

The blue sky that had called me to the gym had now turned purple in preparation for nightfall. It will probably be just as clear tomorrow, I thought.

"It's *hals*, all right." I had been carried into the Uchibori Hospital on the mat, and several doctors were tapping my body with a small hammer and nodding to each other. I did not know anything about medical terminology, but I understood that *hals* refers to any injury of the neck.

"He had better go to Gunma University [Gundai] Hospital. I'll call to tell them he's on the way," said one doctor as he rushed out of the room. A man who appeared to be the head doctor began calling out instructions as an ambulance drove up, and again I was carried out on my mat.

It was the first time I had ever ridden in an ambulance. The siren blared as we rode from Takasaki to Maebashi, where Gundai Hospital was located, and I thought how much louder it always sounded outside an ambulance than it did now from the inside.

A long hallway. I watched as dozens and dozens of fluorescent lights lining the ceiling appeared and then passed over my head. I thought of how my mother would turn pale at the news of my injury. I wondered if she would have enough money to take the train from our little mountain village to Maebashi.

How about the school trip to Lake Haruna? I had also forgotten to total up the scores of some P.E. achievement tests. Oh no, my dirty underwear was still dumped next to the washing machine! That was surely going to surprise somebody! I also worried about my summer bonus money, a large sum I had just received, which I had foolishly stashed away between some cardboard boxes in my closet. There should have been a better place to hide it. Like the fluorescent lights, one thought after another appeared briefly, then disappeared.

I was surprised at the number of white-frocked people in the examining room. As before, they seemed to be tapping me all over with a little hammer.

"Does it hurt?" The doctors asked me the same question again and again. I felt nothing.

"Does it hurt?" Why did they keep saying that? Why? Finally I felt a little pain in my neck. Next I felt something sticking me. They were poking me with a needle, starting at my neck and moving down to my chest. Still, no matter how often I was pricked, I felt nothing below my neck.

"*Hals.*" Here, too, the doctors were whispering that ominous word.

Dozens of hands supported my neck, lifted my body as

if it were made of glass, and moved me to a bed in a private room. A tube was inserted through my nose, and soon oxygen was pouring in. That felt better, but I realized that my injury must be serious if I had to have a machine to help me breathe.

A very pretty young nurse came in and said, "Let's get these clothes off!" She took out a pair of scissors and cut up my shirt. It was a brand new shirt, the same kind worn by the students in the gymnastics club. Soon it was no more than a handful of rags. *Clip, clip, clip.* The sound of the scissors seemed to get louder and louder. It sounded like my shorts were next, and I was chagrined wondering if she was going to cut up my supporter, too!

"Now what have you done to yourself?" My eldest sister and her husband from Isesaki were the first of my family to arrive. The doctor must have told them what my condition was because my sister was trying her hardest to sound alm. It was painfully obvious, but I played along, smiling as cheerfully as I could.

While I was being carried out of the gym, I had realized that my parents would still be working out in their field, and thus impossible to reach, so I had asked to have my sister contacted. I was glad now that I had done so, because it gave me a chance to calm down with her before my parents arrived.

It was two hours later when they finally did come. They had been helping transplant a relative's rice field and had gotten home after 6:30, later than usual. As soon as they had stepped in the door, the telephone had begun to ring—it must have rung dozens of times before then—and they had heard the news about me.

At first my father had planned to come alone. Realizing, however, that my accident had occurred in Takasaki and I had been taken all the way to the university hospital in the next city, my parents had become anxious and decided to go together. Train services do not run late in rural areas, and they had barely managed to catch the last train on the Ashio Line. They had to transfer once at Kiryu, and then go on to Maebashi. My mother had been in such a hurry to leave that she had arrived at the hospital with mud from the rice fields still caked to her shoes.

I was afraid to see my parents' faces. They had been so pleased and proud when I became a teacher. My father and mother had sacrificed their own comfort to put me through college, and I feared that this would be a heavy blow, especially to my mother. I wanted my parents least of all to know how serious my injury was.

I decided to show them what good shape I was really in. Carefully preparing my smile, I tried to put strength in my arms. I tried to move my legs and make myself sit up. Why wouldn't anything move? It was like trying to pedal a bicycle whose chain had slipped; nothing would catch. It was not as painful as it was unbelievable. Until just a few hours ago I had been moving about so freely. In a single second, a second I missed completely, I had acquired a completely different body.

This must be a dream, I thought. This sort of thing happens in dreams all the time. When morning comes, I shall wake up as usual in my little one-room apartment, lying on my dirty *tatami* mats. This white ceiling, these nurses who keep coming and going, and this blood-pressure gauge will all disappear. Then, while I am shoveling down my breakfast, I shall think about what an awful nightmare I'd had. I closed my eyes. Now, when I open them, I should be back in my apartment....

"Sleeping?" It was my mother's voice. Timidly I opened my eyes. I was still in the hospital, all right, and no more than a few minutes had passed. Mother's voice sounded nervous, so I tried to act strong and reassuring.

"Hi! Tired from the long trip? Don't worry, Mom, pull yourself together."

The doctors and nurses came and went in a steady stream all night long, checking my pulse and using their stethoscopes on me. All this made me more and more uneasy about the extent of my injury.

I got no sleep at all until close to dawn, and I managed to keep telling the nurses, who came in every thirty minutes to take my blood pressure, that I was just fine.

June 18

The doctors said I needed blood transfusions. When my college friends who had camped in the hospital hallway all night heard this, they said they would take care of it and headed for the dormitory and the physical education department to round up donors. I wondered what they were feeling. Many of them were P.E. majors headed for careers identical to mine. I realized that it was more than just my own personal problem. I did not want anyone's daily practice sessions to turn into a frightening ordeal. And why did I need a blood transfusion when I was not bleeding anywhere? I shivered, sensing that many more crises were yet to come.

"The eighth graders got off to Haruna on schedule. Don't worry about them, just take it easy!" Several teachers from Kuragano Junior High came by to see me.

I was so tired. I felt as if I had been sleeping with my legs curled up. I asked my sister to straighten them out. She answered that they already were. I asked the same thing over and over. Finally I tried to convince myself that it was all an illusion; but, still, it was as if my legs were rolled as tightly as they had been while turning in the flip. They seemed to be totally disconnected from my will. That alone was enough to fill me with anger and frustration.

"I can't stand it! I can't stand anymore of this!" I screamed at my sister as tears ran down my face.

"Please stop! There's nothing we can do...try to be patient a little longer!" She herself looked ready to cry.

I could not hold back the tears. Around my bed, doctors stood watching me. I did not want them to see such a pitiful-looking face; but the tears continued to flow like water from a broken dam. When I could not take it any longer, I tried to wipe my face with my hand. But where was my hand? I could not even turn my head to hide my tears, and a little round lamp over my face illuminated them mercilessly.

June 19

My sisters were amazed at how many people came to see me.

"Actually, I'm quite well-known," I said proudly, but even I was puzzled by the number of visitors. I knew that there was a connection between that and the seriousness of my condition. This made me feel more uneasy than ever. Who had told everyone? My mountain-climbing pals from Tokyo arrived en masse. One of them said,

"You've finally done it! It was a miracle that you got this far without an accident. You'll be able to rest up for a while anyway, and the mountains will probably enjoy a little peace and quiet, too!"

As soon as they left, a nurse came in with a razor and scissors. "We're going to put you in traction, so I'm going to shave your head." So saying, she began to clip away at my shaggy hair.

Traction meant that they would hang weights from my head, pulling it from behind in order to put my neck bone back in place. But did they have to cut off my hair? While my sister and I were wondering if maybe they were going to glue something to me, several doctors walked in. I heard the humming noise of a motor running just before I realized that they were drilling a hole through the bone of my shiny head!

"Be careful you don't go too far!" joked the doctors to each other. Soon there were two holes, and the smell of drilled bone pervaded the room. They put metal fixtures in the two holes and hung weights from them. With these and more weights hung from a pulley attached to my bed, my head was pulled tight. As unpleasant as that sounds, I felt no pain anywhere. My neck even felt a little better. I was glad just to know it was going to be properly reset. Starting the next day, the doctor told me, they would begin to add more weight.

Whenever I clenched my teeth I felt a metallic resonance all over my face.

"I feel like Astro Boy," I said, gnashing my teeth together a couple of times for the doctor.

According to him, the neck is made up of seven vertebrae. Of those, my fourth and fifth were out of place, and the nerves running through them were causing irregularities.

June 20

My mountain-climbing buddies spent the night, some in the hall and some in their cars in the hospital parking lot. As they weren't allowed to sit with me in my room, they relayed their messages: "Hang in there. We're staying right here with you!" It was greatly encouraging just knowing such good friends were close by.

It became harder to breathe. I would take a deep breath and only get about half of the air into my lungs. My chest felt as though it were being strapped down by an iron belt. I had to take two or three gulps for every word I wanted to say. Soon, I was concentrating all of my energy on breathing.

Then, irritated by the oxygen tube, my nose began to bleed profusely. The doctor stuffed gauze in my nose and put an oxygen mask over my mouth; still, no matter how hard I tried, I was not getting enough air. The harder I tried, the more excruciating it became. How long was this going to last, I wondered. Soon, I was completely worn out.

Suddenly the realization of how critical my condition was crossed my mind like a dark shadow. I kept my eyes focused on my parents and sisters. How lonely I felt!

Death!? Is it this easy to die? It can't be! I was fine until just a few days ago! I'm healthier and twice as strong as anybody! I'm young! Death is something that I do not need to think about yet! Every time I gasped for air, I repeated to myself my refusal to die.

Doctors came in one after the other. They said that my whole body had become cyanotic. I did not quite understand what that meant, but it seemed that the lack of air was making purple spots break out all over my body.

One of my earliest memories is a dim recollection of a wide stairway and a long hallway. I am playing by myself, going up and down the stairway. At the top of the stairs is another long hallway. I want to walk down it, and take a few steps. But I get scared and go back down the stairs. Then I go up again and walk a little farther down the hallway. A roomful of people are sitting with their backs to me. There are a lot of nails on the wall, with brooms and cleaning rags hanging from them. I get down on all fours and crawl back and forth along the wall. As a child, I could never remember when or where this was.

When I got a little older and linked this memory with a story my sister told me, I decided it must have been an elementary school. When I was five, Mother was bedridden with pneumonia for a long time. My second-eldest sister took me to school with her so that she could watch me. During class, when I got tired of playing in the back of the classroom, I would go and play on the stairs, she had told me.

"My teacher and all my classmates loved having you there and always played with you." My sister had smiled at the memory.

Memories of my childhood went through my head in rapid succession: my mother took my hand, and we went to the village Bon Festival. Red lanterns gently swaying; men, with shining faces and headbands tied across their foreheads, singing old songs called *yagibushi*. The rhythm from the band of hand drums and bells seemed to swell up from under the earth. The drums excited me, but I was too shy to join the circle of dancers.

Another memory: the village youth group had a talent show. My eldest sister was dressed in a beautiful kimono and danced holding a fan. I left my mother and elbowed my way up front for a better view. In the circle of pale yellow light, my sister was so lovely that somehow I thought she had turned into somebody else. This thought saddened me, and I rushed back to be with my mother. I could not find her anywhere! I searched for her face among those lit up by the dim light of the lanterns. Tired out, I left the crowd and found myself near the temple. The darkness of night that enveloped it was like the overlapping shadows of thousands of ghosts.

Why did these scenes keep coming back to me?

I was born the fifth of seven children and was to a great extent raised by my elder sisters. Perhaps I was remembering my childhood because they were by my side now.

I had a desperate desire to know what I was like when I

was small. My sisters seemed taken aback when I asked them to tell me stories about myself, but they began searching their memories.

"Let me see. What happened when you were a baby?" My second-eldest sister started to speak but did not seem able to continue.

"How about the time when I fell asleep in the leaves?" I tried to nudge her on.

"You remember that story?"

"I think I heard it once a long time ago."

"Well...you were never a nervous baby. All anybody had to do was touch your eyelids, and you'd go right to sleep." She spoke as if she were telling a child a bedtime story. I closed my eyes, still able to see the brightness of the ceiling lights through my eyelids, and tried to imagine how my sister's small hands must have felt.

"Mother and Father were collecting fallen leaves to use as fertilizer, and we'd all climbed up the mountain to help. We ended up playing, of course, and you fell asleep. We had a great time covering you with leaves, then got so involved in our game that we forgot all about you. When we realized what had happened, we'd lost you! Masae and I panicked and began searching through all the leaves. We finally found you, sleeping blissfully among them."

The me I didn't know; a baby sleeping so peacefully. My parents were poor, but what a loving upbringing I had had! Could it now end so easily?

No! I suddenly felt as if everything I had done since then no longer mattered. I would renounce it all—if I could just go back one more time and fall asleep among those leaves!

CHAPTER TWO

Mother Joins Me

June 22 to August 30, 1970

(Gentian)

From the Doctor's Report

June 22: Owing to respiratory difficulty, we performed a tracheotomy and applied a respirator. (As the patient was on the verge of death, the operation was a race against asphyxia.) After the operation, his fever continued; other complications included pneumonia and urinary tract infection. (He was maintained at this time by the respirator as well as by his own exceptional stamina.)

Note: The human neck is made up of seven vertebrae; motor and other nerves in this area control movements of the arms, legs, and other parts of the body. His fourth vertebra suffered a fracture-dislocation. Since the first through third vertebrae control movements from the shoulders up, there was no problem in that area, but the rest of his body was completely paralyzed. Most people with similar injuries die of suffocation. The nerves which control the diaphragm, however, are just above the fourth vertebra which, in his case, escaped damage. Thus, he could resort to abdominal breathing. However, as he is still only getting about half the air necessary for a normal person, his strength is diminishing, leaving him in a critical state.

From Mother's Reminiscences

We were saved by the respirator. After the tracheotomy, however, Tomihiro broke out in a high fever, and his blood pressure and pulse became erratic. Because of the seriousness of his condition, no one was able to get a wink of sleep. When we tried to cool off his body with ice, it was amazing how fast it melted. Phlegm kept clogging up his windpipe, and it had to be removed by suction. It looked so painful and had to be done so often that I could not bear to watch. Tomihiro's fever continued for two days and he was weakening, so I spent the night watching him and all his apparatus, praying that his heart would not give out.

I heard that this respirator had been borrowed from another department; it came in a big box and had many knobs. It hissed loudly as it pumped air at regular intervals. I breathed in and out along with the hissing sound, thinking that I would gladly sacrifice my own body if it would save his life.

Of course, his body was immobile, and his head was fixed so as not to move an inch. After the tracheotomy, he could not speak at all; he could only stare at the ceiling day after day. I was tormented by the very fact that he was conscious; just being near him I broke into tears, knowing that he must be having terrible, unfathomable thoughts.

After about a month his lungs recovered, his breathing became deeper, and his condition stabilized. Even so, when I raised his body even a little to sponge him down, all the color drained out of his face, and his eyes told me how badly he felt. The slightest movement made breathing difficult, it seemed. The nurses, however, told me that I should start exercising his arms if possible. We also tried turning him on his side a little.

Phlegm still clogged his throat, and sometimes I had to clear it as often as once every hour. It was impossible to sleep easily at night. When I saw a small change for the better, though, I forgot the pain. I just kept praying that his arms and legs would soon be able to move again.

June 22

It was midnight, but the lamp over my head was brightly lit. There was a dark stain in the middle of the light that looked like a vacant face. Each breath I took required the same deliberate effort that I made when counting out push-ups, and I was completely worn out. If I took a rest from breathing once in a while, the faces of my sisters peeking over at me would become blurred. Mother was not feeling well and had gone home. As if to encourage me on, the people in the room all synchronized their breathing with mine. Then somebody said that my chest was convulsing, and ran out of the room. Almost immediately a doctor rushed in.

"I'm so tired," my faint voice begged for help.

After a few minutes, four or five other doctors came in and explained what they were about to do.

"We're going to perform a tracheotomy. You won't be able to talk for some time, but you'll feel better right away."

The doctors were anesthetists and ear, nose, and throat specialists. They covered my eyes, but I could hear the sound of metal on metal. They opened a hole in my throat and inserted a tube. Then there was a sound, *shoo*..., and, with a strong force, air was thrust into my chest. The machine sent air in the same way I would if I were breathing normally. I could relax and let the machine breathe for me. I felt better immediately. What a wonderful gadget, I thought. Then my built-up fatigue overwhelmed me, and I became sleepy. I could not speak at all.

Humans are an unsatisfied lot, I thought. Having been saved from the pain of breathing (or rather, the pain of death), I was now tormented by the fact that I was unable to speak. I could not move my body, nod my head, or say a word; in other words, there was no way to communicate my feelings. People always say that the eyes can be as expressive as words, but when it came down to it, my eyes were not very helpful at all. It was hard enough not being able to make myself understood, but it was just as bad not being able to do anything. Before, even though I could not move, I could pass the time talking. Deprived now of all forms of communication, I had nothing to do all day but stare at the ceiling and blink my eyes. An amazing thing was that after I lost my voice, people seemed to have the impression that I had also gone deaf. Even my sisters stopped talking to me.

The only sound in my room was the heavy resonance of the respirator. As if they had been hypnotized, my sisters all breathed along with it. I also realized that visitors were being kept out. I would hear what sounded like a familiar voice just outside my door, but then the person would turn around and leave without coming in. That made me lonely. Lonelier than ever.

My father and mother, younger sister and brother, and my four elder sisters and their husbands all took turns taking care of me. None of them was getting much sleep, and they all looked exhausted. I could not help feeling responsible.

After classes ended, the teachers from Kuragano would come and stay for three of four hours to give my family some time to rest.

"I washed the clothes you left in the caretaker's room. There sure was a lot of it!" Mrs. Muraki, the school nurse, came to sit with me. She said that the students were amazed at the great amount of underwear hung out to dry.

A friend who had been in the gymnastics club with me in high school and college was given special permission to visit. Since we had known each other so long, I thought that even if I could not speak he would know what I was thinking. I looked into his eyes and tried to send a message.

Sorry to trouble you, but thank you for coming all the way over here today. I'm so glad to see you. He remained silent, watching me closely. I felt that our thoughts had met and intertwined.

Hoshino, be tough! You've got to get better! His eyes gently told mine. He understands, I thought. I was deeply moved.

But the next moment, he turned to my sister and asked in a choked voice, "Is something wrong with his head, too?"

I had to find a way to tell people what I was thinking.

The only way was for people to read my lips. I started opening and closing my mouth, trying to get attention. Then, carefully forming each sound with my lips, I made a word. My sisters opened their mouths wide, copying mine, and tried to say what they thought I wanted to say. But all they managed was an incoherent jumble of sounds. At first I was frustrated, but eventually it became funny. All I could do was lie there like a dead weight anyway, and this game became my only recreation.

If there happened to be four people in the room, all four would open their mouths as wide as possible, mimicking me, making the different sounds, "Ahh...," "Ohh...." Anyone listening would have thought it a weird chorus of sorts, but they were all dead serious. Their seriousness was a powerful thing, and after a few days of this, my sisters were reading my lips fairly accurately.

Then I got an idea!

If they made a chart with the characters for the fifty sounds of the Japanese language, and I could indicate the ones I wanted, they could understand me better and faster, I thought. Still, I had no way to convey this idea.

One day, my third-eldest sister finally grasped the idea and made the chart. Even if they pointed to each character in turn, however, I could not nod when they got to the one I wanted. After thinking a while, I decided to make a big smile that said, *That's it!* It took a great effort to make my face look cheery when I was feeling so awful, but there was no other way. After a while, I realized that I could cluck my tongue. Then my sisters divided the characters into several rows so that I could first indicate the row, and then the sound I wanted in that row. This way, we did not have to go through all the sounds each time.

Looking back, it seems silly that it took so long for us to think up such a simple system. All of us were much too caught up in the fear of death.

I had to be fed through a tube that conveyed liquid food directly to my stomach because the action of chewing moved my jaws, which affected my neck injury. After meals I never felt as if I had eaten. I wanted very much to chew something. I opened and closed my mouth several times, and my eldest sister guessed what I wanted.

"We'll give you something to suck on, but *no chewing*!"

She put a piece of gum a little ways into my mouth. I could taste it with the tip of my tongue—the temptation was too great! I tried to get it out of my sister's hand, and started champing on it. She went pale and tried to push her finger in farther to get the gum out. I refused to let her take it and bit down hard. No matter how much it hurt, she refused to let go. I didn't care what it took. I wanted that gum, even if I had to chew my sister's finger to bits!

Is that what humans can do when they are not allowed to eat? When I finally calmed down and thought about it, I was frightened by what I was capable of.

To make myself understood took forever. Once we got used to the chart, we went from short words to longer, more complicated matters. But when we came to the end of a long sentence, my mother or my sisters would often forget what the beginning had been, for which they apologized again and again.

In addition to making communication possible, this was also a way for me to kill time; so even when my sisters made mistakes, it was still fun.

I got permission to drink any fluid I liked while the feeding tube was in my mouth, so I asked for juice. My sister got this mixed up with "shoes" (which is almost the same as "juice" in written Japanese).

"He wants to wear shoes! Oh, dear."

"Listen, Tomihiro, when you're better you can wear shoes. I'll put them right here by your bed." Saying this, someone picked up a pair of shoes to show me.

When the lamp was too bright, I signaled *denki* ("electric light"). Someone would get up and look out the window.

"Looks like it's cloudy." (The word for "weather" is *tenki*.)

It was times like these when I would use my chart to scold them:

"Get serious, idiot!"

June 27

The tenth day. We had all reached our limits. My

sisters and mother were going without much sleep, so the chief nurse let them use an empty room to rest in.

My body was full of different fixtures: a feeding tube from my mouth to my stomach, the respirator attached to the hole in my throat, IV tubes in my arms and legs, weights hanging from my head, and another tube carrying away my body wastes. Nurses were in and out of my room all the time to check on each machine, as well as the gauze in my nose to stop the bleeding. They also had to clean the phlegm out of my throat and take my temperature and blood pressure. I was certainly a troublesome patient.

Dr. Nishimura, who was new at Gundai Hospital, stayed by my side all night whenever he was on duty.

"The human body is made so that if one part is having trouble the other parts become stronger to help it out," he said.

Seeing all these people working so hard for me, I felt my own responsibility not to give up! Still, whenever I thought about the future, it seemed closed and bleak. All I wanted was for the present to pass.

At some point, clucking my tongue once came to mean "my head hurts." The only part of my body that retained any feeling was making up for the rest by becoming especially sensitive. My head, pulled by a seven-kilogram weight, rested on a doughnut-shaped cushion of cotton and gauze, which was placed on a board and pulley used for traction. My head was not allowed to move even a millimeter. Since I was in the same position all the time, the cushion would become flattened out and the board bared so that my head pressed directly against it, causing a splitting headache. For relief, I clucked my tongue once, and the doctor would come and raise my head a little.

Clucking twice meant "What time is it?" I asked this so many times that whoever was with me would nearly go crazy. This was understandable, as I often asked every ten minutes. To me, those ten minutes felt like four or five hours.

Night was worse. From about 11 p.m. I would start wishing for morning to come. It was not as though I was going to hear any good news the next morning; but whenever the window began turning pale white, I would feel pure delight.

Morning—no matter what the circumstances—is this not a time that provides at least a moment of hope? Because I had no cause to look forward to the future, I was able to rejoice unconditionally in the light of the morning. That light was many times brighter than it had been when I was healthy. It was like morning seen from a mountaintop, breaking through a sea of clouds.

Ever since I was small I had been robust and full of strength. I had made better use of my physical power than most people might, and I hated to lose to anybody. In junior high I had been in the track club, running everyday as far and as fast as I possibly could. A boy from a little mountain village, I had taken first place in a prefectural athletic meet.

> From the farthest side of my memories
>   a solitary boy is running this way
> It might be me
>   the day I got my first pair of white sneakers
>   swelled with joy
>   letting the grass stain the white canvas
> Running towards today

My high school was a public boy's school. I was neither good at nor interested in classroom studies, but during gym period and after school at club, I would suddenly come to life. The rings hanging from the gym ceiling were a novelty to me, so I joined the gymnastics club. At the same time, I was interested in mountain climbing. Since it is normal for Japanese students to belong to only one club, I joined gymnastics; but I went to the mountaineering clubroom almost every day and participated in all of their outings. The time I spent with them meant time away from gymnastics. I was often scolded by the coach, but I could not give up mountain climbing. Considering me one of their own, club members even gave me a farewell party when I graduated.

I majored in physical education in college because I wanted to continue gymnastics. And I became a physical education teacher because I wanted a job that would let me use my body and move around as much as I wanted to.

I was already twenty-four years old. I had learned many things and had lots of experiences. All of these had become flesh and blood, and made me what I was. For example, during college I had gone out of my way to put myself into extreme situations.

With only an umbrella, a sleeping bag, and a little money, I had gone to places I had never been, sleeping under the eaves of shrines, in drainpipes, and on beaches, and asking for food as a beggar would. Wanting to test my own limits, I had also spent days wandering through the mountains.

Even in gymnastics I had been drawn to dangerous feats. As for mountaineering, I had become entranced by rock climbing, a pastime always taking one to the brink of death. By putting myself into dangerous situations, I had forced myself to become stronger. And I thought I had become strong.

The strength I had built up through those experiences, however, was not sustaining me now that I was unable to move or speak. Rather, it was as though twenty-four years of experience were somehow reduced to a hopelessness that stretched into eternity. This thought seemed to destroy all of my strength, turning it instead into an all-consuming despair that tore me apart.

What was keeping me alive? I was not doing anything

myself. It was my parents who gave birth to me, my brothers and sisters who were raised with me, my friends, the teachers who worked with me, the doctors, the respirator, and the students who had folded a thousand paper cranes for luck and were praying for my recovery.

I was as naked as I had been at birth. I could neither live by my own strength nor did I believe in anything that could comfort me. There was nothing to keep me alive except what other people gave me.

Exactly what was the point of all those things that I had thought made me strong? Where had that strength gone? During those days spent staring at the ceiling, I was able to think rationally about my past. Perhaps all I had done to become stronger had had the opposite effect. Somewhere along the way it had, rather, made me aware of my weakness. Since I had not wanted to recognize this part of myself, I had talked myself into believing that I had become strong.

I had never wanted to believe that I was weak, nor did I want other people to see this side of me. That was why I had been drawn compulsively to sports and other risks. All I had really done was to cover up and cloak my weakness with a garment called strength. Now I had nothing to conceal or hide my weakness with. Not being able to move, I could not run away from it, nor could I say anything to gloss it over. Perhaps I had returned to my true state of being.

I was afraid of the approach of sleepless nights, even though I was in bed all the time and found it hard to tell night from day because doctors and nurses were constantly in and out of my room. People often say that you can sleep if you count, so I tried that; but when I reached a thousand, even two thousand, I was still wide awake, just more tired. I imagined sheep after sheep jumping over a fence, then I tried counting raindrops that I could hear outside, but nothing worked. I even went through the multiplication tables. Then I remembered that I had memorized some poems.

I had been fond of poems since elementary-school days. I had even written some poems myself. When in high school, I had read with enthusiasm the works of famous poets and had memorized several by Sakutaro Hagiwara, Tatsuji Miyoshi, Michizo Tachihara, and some Chinese poets. Reciting these poems was the only power I had left to my disposal. One by one, I tirelessly repeated to myself as many poems as I could remember. And what had happened? At some point I began to fall asleep easily and peacefully.

The beauty and grandeur of the Chinese poems unraveled the threads of uneasiness and desolation that were tangling up my feelings. Tatsuji Miyoshi's "Along a Temple Path" sent a gentle breeze and strewed delicately-fragrant flower petals inside my heavy and closed heart, so that I found myself walking slowly in the world of poetry: playing, then pleasantly tired, and drifting off to sleep. I felt at that time that I had discovered the true beauty of those poems. Even the ones I had previously thought of as no more than short columns of characters now came to life and permeated my being.

I was happy just to discover that I had within me even a small capacity to comfort myself. I decided that if I was lucky enough to survive I would learn more of such life-giving verses.

June 30

The doctor in charge of me, Dr. Kiryu, charged into my room. He was an outspoken man who roared at the flustered nurses but was always gentle with me.

"According to the X-rays, your vertebrae are right back in place!" He was obviously pleased with the news. It was only twelve days since I had been put in traction. The weight was up to seven-and-a-half kilograms, and I had been told that it would be necessary to add more weight and that it would take a much longer time. The bones in my neck were already back in place!

"Do you feel any difference?" He beamed and waited a few moments for me to say something. I wanted to answer, but I could not speak. Finally, he remembered.

"Oh! That's right, I forgot." I was happy, but he was even more elated at my rapid progress. Now they would decrease the weight bit by bit. The entrance to the long, directionless road I knew I had to take showed just the faintest glimmer of light. I wanted to cling to it.

July 17

Dr. Yamato, the anesthetist, came to my room every day to take a blood sample or to readjust the respirator. He always cheered me up.

"You've improved quite a bit. Just hold out a little longer!"

I was warmed by his kindness. I and whoever was with me always looked forward to hearing his heavy footsteps on the stairway. He looked trustworthy in his operating-room outfit: blue-green shirt, baggy pants, matching cap, and the mask hanging from his neck.

On this day he changed the tube in my throat. It was a plastic, L-shaped tube, about as thick as a forefinger. This tube was connected to the respirator. When he took it out of my throat, *hew- hew-*, air came out of the hole, and for a few moments I was able to breathe by myself. It was a very ordinary, simple thing, but I was thrilled.

"Bet you'd like to talk once in a while." Dr. Yamato plugged up the hole in my throat with gauze.

"All right, say something."

I was at a loss. It had been a month since I had last used my voice. It was like having a microphone thrust in front of me; as much as I wanted to talk, I did not know what to say. Many words swirled around in my head, but none

would come out of my mouth. Till now the time had
passed so slowly, but I was afraid this moment would fly
by. I could not wait any longer.

"Ahhh, er..., hmmn, testing—one, two, three!"

There was a burst of laughter; my mother, sisters, the
doctor, and the nurses were all laughing. It was the first
time I had heard laughter in that room. The heavy, stuffy
air of the private room vibrated with the sound. I wanted
to believe that even one little change would lead to hope.
I yearned for the brighter day it might bring along with it.

My third-eldest sister came back from shopping looking
happy about something. It had been drizzling since
morning, and the air had become very humid. Seeking
some sort of relief, she had tried to buy some paper fans at
a store in front of the hospital, but there were none to be
had. A woman whom she had never met before had
overheard her talking to the clerk and spoke up,

"I have some at home. Please wait here a minute."

Then she ran to her bicycle and pedaled off, returning
soon with three fancy paper fans.

My sister was almost in tears over the kindness of this
unknown person in an unfamiliar town. The breeze of the
fan calmed me, but more than that, I realized how
refreshing the kindness and love of people could be.

"Don't forget these fans, Tomihiro," my sister said to
me. The person who gave them to us would probably
never know how much the breeze of those three fans

soothed and gladdened people passing so many days of solitude and anxiety in a hospital.

July 23

Every day I practiced breathing on my own, and finally I managed to do it without the respirator. The thought that perhaps I could not do it had been strange and frightening. The doctor changed my L-shaped tube from a plastic to a metal one. The corner of the tube had a hole through which air was released to my mouth, allowing me to speak a little bit. People could now understand immediately what I wanted to say! How convenient it is to be able to talk. What a blessing! No one had to read my lips or use the character chart any more!

The first night, I talked until late with two high-school friends, Arai and Oyama. It was as if a dam had been broken. These two lived an hour away in Kiryu, but they came to the hospital every day. Besides looking after me, they were also concerned about my family, bringing food as well as other daily necessities. Now, it felt as if I was trying to make up for all the silent days when we could only stare at each other. And they were as happy as if they had been the ones who had been unable to talk for so long.

I had thought that I had lost everything, but I still had my sisters and my good friends. We talked and talked and talked—about high-school days, about the times

when we had gone to the mountains together, about
Oyama's brother who had died mountain climbing, and
on and on. I talked so much that I broke out in a fever
after they left.

July 29

The doctors informed me that they were going to
remove the metal fixtures that kept my head in traction
and turn me on my side. It would be the first time for me
to change position in forty-two days. A soft, thick, cotton-
filled cloth was tied around my neck. Then a large
number of doctors and nurses gathered around. Placing
my face on a pillow, they synchronized their motions with
a "One-two-three!" and turned me on my side. The
people behind me cheered and congratulated me. Patients
who are confined to their beds almost always get
bedsores, but I had none. Everyone was surprised and
pleased. They said that I had been spared the awful
bedsores thanks to careful treatment, my own strength,
and the air mat placed on my bed from the time I had
arrived at the hospital.

When one stays in the same position in bed for a long
time, the blood cannot circulate through parts of the body
which have direct contact with the mattress, and the flesh
actually rots. Patients with injuries similar to mine
sometimes die not from their original wounds, but from
bedsores.

Now that I was turned, however, I did not feel like I was on my side at all. The ceiling seemed to collapse behind my ears only to be replaced by the wall facing me. The doctors and nurses suddenly looked as though they were walking on the wall. My head started to spin, and breathing became difficult. Even though so many people had gone to so much trouble to turn me, I had to be put on my back again after just a few moments. After a month-and-a-half with no more than the ceiling and the upper walls in my field of vision, my sense of equilibrium had become warped. I was told that I would be put on my side for a few minutes a day until I got used to it. I wondered what color the floor was. What shape were the legs of the nurses? I must have seen them, but I could not recall them at all.

Otaki, a year behind me in high school, had been in the mountain climbing club in which I had been an active participant. So when Otaki became a senior and the club president, he had invited me to participate in their fall and winter camps. Having already graduated from high school, I sorely missed my mountain-climbing friends, most of whom had gone off to Tokyo, so I was glad to accept Otaki's invitation. I went with him to climb Mt. Tanigawa, a dangerous but favorite place of ours. Other trips followed even after he entered college in Tokyo.

Otaki's loyalty and sincerity towards his seniors in school was a rare thing. He always carried the heavier pack, ate the worst food, and, when we had to bivouac on a cliff partway up a mountain, gave me the more comfortable spot. The autumn preceding, the two of us had gone to Japan's Northern Alps to climb the D face of Byobuiwa and the east face of Maehotakadake. Otaki stopped by to see me in the hospital after his summer camp. In his small but heavy-looking pack, he must have had his *haken* and *karabiner* and other mountain-climbing equipment. I knew he had carried his well-worn climbing shoes into my room, because I heard the heavy sound of them being dropped to the floor.

With his suntanned face, windblown hair, and heavy wool shirt, he brought with him the smell of rocks warmed by the summer sun. He stood by my side, staring at my face, not saying a word. He looked as if he could not believe what he was seeing. I gazed back at him, also unable to speak. Suddenly he turned and left my room. There was a loud thud outside the door, followed by someone's call for a nurse. I could hear several pairs of feet running down the hallway, and then silence.

What had happened to him? I waited anxiously. Thirty or forty minutes later he came back and stood by my bed with his head lowered.

"Sorry. I fainted, and they let me rest in another room for a while."

His face, drained of blood, looked even darker than before.

August 30

The doctors took out a rubber tube, called an indwelling catheter, that had been inserted in my bladder through the urethra. Having no feeling or control, I could not urinate by myself. But, I was told, when the bladder becomes full, it should be able to contract and empty itself automatically.

My mother positioned a bedpan near me and took up a watchful position. For thirty minutes, an hour..., we waited breathlessly, as if we were about to receive a wonderful gift.

"You know, most people with the same kind of injury learn to do it for themselves. You will be able to, too," said one of the nurses.

I was finding it harder and harder to believe.

Maybe my injury is different and I shall not be able to manage it, I thought. Two hours, three hours. Sweat broke out on my forehead. My abdomen had hardened somewhat, my mother said. A nurse came running and began pressing my stomach. Still nothing would come out. The nurse increased her efforts.

I wonder how long it took. We waited, holding our breath, and then, at last, we heard a little dribbling sound.

"I think I heard something." The nurse peeked under the blanket.

"You did it! You did it!"

Listening to my mother's exhilarated voice, I shouted to myself, *Banzai!*

Unfortunately, I had no sensation of urinating; but I took hope in the fact that, even though this action was totally disconnected from my own will, my body was gradually learning how to depend on its own natural capabilities.

This happiness, however, was short-lived. Every two or three hours, day and night, my mother had to scurry around with a bedpan, and each time she had to press and rub my abdomen until it seemed my skin might come off. Only rarely could I urinate naturally. Sometimes my abdomen would swell up in the middle of the night, and Mother would have to work on it for as long as ten minutes. As I had no indication whether or not my bladder was full, she could not sleep well at night because she had to check my abdomen every so often.

There was a metal tube in the hole of my throat, and sometimes the phlegm would build up in the insertion. This phlegm had to be removed by suction. Mother had never had much contact with machines; but now she would switch on the suction machine, put the attached rubber tube into my throat, and clean out the phlegm. Her motions were very smooth; in fact, she was better at it than any of the nurses.

This was the woman who had fainted several times just looking at that hole when it was first opened. Day and night, she performed these tasks with which she had had no experience. The more I watched her do it and observed her progress, the more sorrowful I became. Often, after a night when I was in pain, we welcomed the dawn without having slept a wink. Patients can sleep during the day, but those who take care of patients are not allowed a moment's rest. For one thing, there was no place in my room for her to sleep. At night she fit a borrowed cot into the narrow space by my bed, but she could not rest easily there.

How long would it continue like this? Had it been a fixed period of time with the final day marked on the calendar, it would have been different, but I had taken my mother on a journey with no end in sight.

My little mother seemed smaller than ever.

CHAPTER THREE

Those Who Are Heavy Burdened

September 1970 to February 1972

(Daffodil)

From the Doctor's Report

The patient's condition remained stable for a while, but at midnight on December 9 he started groaning in his sleep and lost consciousness. His breathing stopped several times for two to three minutes at a stretch. His pupils were dilated, and he had two convulsive fits. Artificial respiration was applied with no effect.

From Mother's Reminiscences

Moving Tomihiro to a larger room provided a change of atmosphere. Although his condition was hopeless, he seemed more cheerful and ate well. I tried to comfort myself by telling myself that he was getting better and waited hopefully for each new day.

In November, we put a wedge under the upper half of his body to raise him a bit. All it took to bring on a high fever, however, was for his head to fall from his pillow, and this made it impossible for me to relax. Often he was unable to urinate for three or four hours. At such times his abdomen swelled and his lips turned blue. Then he would vomit and lose his appetite. This kind of thing happened often. Small problems that usually would not matter at all were serious enough to endanger his life. After he pulled through each crisis, however, it seemed as though he would suddenly make great progress, and we would become optimistic again.

All the other patients in his room were very cheerful and agreeable. Having them there was wonderful for our morale.

On December 9, at 12:45 a.m., Tomihiro let out a strange cry. I awoke to find his eyes rolled back, and his hands and feet grown cold. I called his name, but he did not answer. A doctor rushed in and did everything he could, but with no effect. He then told me to contact the family immediately. Was it going to end like this? I shook all over, unable to find the phone numbers in my address book.

September 1

I was moved, bed and all, into a large six-person room and given a spot next to the window. It was much sunnier there than in my private room which faced north.

I had not seen the sky since I had entered the hospital, and that day there was a vivid, blue autumn sky. Plantain leaves swayed leisurely in the fresh breeze. The leaves of the *keyaki* trees beyond them made a soft rustling sound.

The hospital in which I had spent so many agonizing days had been under this bright, beautiful sky all the time!

The five-story building on the other side of the *keyaki* trees looked like another hospital ward. Three or four children, their heads all bandaged in a similar manner, were leaning out the window, calling someone in a loud voice. Opposite my bed in the same room were three women talking to each other and laughing so hard they just about fell out of bed.

"This room is a lot of fun, and sunny, too. You can see the sky. Your appetite will get better in no time," said the nurse as she adjusted my suction machine. Even the nurses seemed prettier and more animated than they had before.

Several new patients came to my room, middle-aged to older women who were going to be fitted with artificial hip joints. For years and years they had had to walk with a limp, and they had all endured a good deal of pain.

Only recently had this surgery been introduced to

Japan, and, despite the seriousness of the operation, all the ladies were cheerful and good-humored, but when any one of them began telling the story of her life, they all cried together. They had all had similar trials because of their shared handicap.

On my side of the room was a man in critical condition who had been carried to the hospital after one of his arms and a leg had been severed by a mining truck. Next to me was a high-school student who was going to have one leg amputated because of a tumor. He had been a long-distance runner. The night before his operation, I watched him through the darkness as he sat on his bed, gazing at his leg and stroking it with both hands.

Every day the radio brought us lively reports of the World Exposition being held in Osaka. We heard about the thousands, the tens of thousands, lined up in front of the pavilions from each country. There were broadcasts from the Festival Square filled with singing voices. All this was happening in Japan where we, too, were.

Although I had some idea of the seriousness of my condition, I could not help thinking that my paralyzed body was heading toward recovery now that I had been moved to a larger room and no longer needed either the respirator or the catheter. Following my accident, my body became extremely debilitated, causing the nails on my hands and feet to dry and flake off. As I grew stronger, however, pale-pink healthy nails began growing in underneath. I wished that the rest of my body would respond in the same manner. And I was encouraged by visitors who told me stories they had heard of people with similar injuries who had been cured and gone back to work.

On Thursdays and Fridays, the professors of Gundai Medical School came to examine the patients. Five or six of their students would gather around each bed to look at X-rays and listen to descriptions of our illnesses and present conditions. While I joked with the nurses—"A good-looking man photographs well, even on X-rays!"—I listened carefully to what the professors were saying. They discussed all important matters in German or English, so I could not understand them at all. I decided that the parts I could not understand must be the least hopeful.

My friends and my sisters, people in my room, there were plenty of people who said I would recover; not one who said I would not.

I am sure they could not say that. Or else they simply could not believe that I had declined from such a healthy condition to my present state. Regardless of how much hope I chose to harbor, my body obstinately refused to move—no matter how many days or how many months passed.

I knew that neither despair nor optimism would make any difference; my body would never move again. I did not want to face it, but it was a sad reality that I had to come to terms with.

The boy next to me, Sakurai, whose leg had been amputated, was the first friend I made in the hospital. Following his operation he said nothing about pain, injustice or frustration, and even managed to show a cheerful face. He often sent requests to an FM radio station and looked forward to hearing his name announced over the air. Every once in a while he would send in requests for me so that I could hear my name, too.

Listening for our songs to be played, I gradually learned to enjoy the music of the Beatles and other rock music for which I had never had much appreciation before. It was around that time that the hospital began segregating rooms by sex. The women patients were moved out of our room, and other patients, all male, with unusual injuries and illnesses were moved in.

Toward the end of November, the upper half of my body was raised for the first time by putting a wedge under my back. I was lifted only about ten degrees; but having been flat on my back for so long, I felt like I was sitting straight up. My unsupported head fell heavily on my shoulders.

Using this wedge every day to accustom me to sitting up was the doctor's order, but I would pass out if raised with the least suddenness.

December 9
I awoke in the middle of the night to find several

doctors and nurses standing around my bed. It seemed late, and I thought it was a little strange, especially when I noticed that, among them, there were doctors whom I rarely saw at all.

"Thank goodness, Tomihiro! What a relief!" my mother cried in an elated voice. I had no idea what she was so happy about, but realized that something must have happened.

I heard a hollow bubbling sound over my head. Somebody must be getting oxygen. No! The tube was inserted right into my throat. What had happened? Someone said,

"Can you hear me? How do you feel?"

I recognized the voice of a professor and saw other faces looking down at me. It had been a long time since I had had the attention of so many doctors and nurses, and I felt rather pleased. Gradually my legs began to tingle, and the feeling seemed to spread to the upper half of my body. Then I was overcome with an intense loneliness such as I had never felt before.

"My legs are numb...." Listening to my own voice, I lost consciousness.

The next time my eyes opened, I saw my parents, three of my elder sisters, and my younger sister and brother. After a few minutes, my other sister and her husband arrived from Hanno City in Saitama Prefecture after a three-hour taxi ride.

I had no idea what was going on. When my mother

explained the next day, it was enough to make my hair stand on end.

At about midnight I had given a short yell. My mother awoke and asked what I wanted, and, receiving no answer, she checked me more closely and found that I was not breathing. She hastily called a nurse, who then called the doctor on duty. The doctor ran in and inserted the tube of a handpump-operated respirator into the hole that had been left open in my throat. He tried again and again to pump air into my lungs before he advised my mother,

"Contact your family immediately."

There were several favorable conditions, however, which finally led to my recovery. The hole from the tracheotomy was still open. Even though it was the middle of the night, several doctors were available. More than anything, my mother had realized in time that something was wrong. I felt that my life was something glistening brightly, separated from the rest of me.

Sakurai came to my side.

"I was so worried. I thought for sure we'd lost you."

January 1, 1971

The new year came to our hospital room. We patients wondered if perhaps the nurses would come to work wearing beautiful kimonos; but no, they wore their usual white uniforms. They came to our door and wished us a happy New Year, however, and we all returned the greeting.

Being greeted and being able to greet was a joy.

It had been eight years since I had spent the first of January under the same roof with my mother. I loved mountains, and I took pride in my custom of welcoming the new year perched on a snow-covered peak. Whether in a tent half-buried in snow or at a ski resort where I had a part-time job, I felt superior because I did not spend the New Year's holidays in the same way everybody else did. Oh no, I was different from all those who nonchalantly sat around drinking *sake*, warm and cozy, safe inside a house.

How about this New Year's Day? There was no doubt that I was not feeling particularly cozy. There was no *sake*. On top of that, I could not move a muscle. This had to be my most extraordinary one yet. My celebration was in my usual, austere manner, but this time my feeling of superiority had vanished.

My sister in Isesaki brought some traditional holiday dishes, and they were good. As I ate, I thought of the warmth of my home: the soft, gooey rice cakes cooked over the fire; the greens of the *kadomatsu* made of pine and bamboo and set in front of the house to assure safety during the new year; the veranda, with thawing ice on the eaves, glistening in the morning light as it yielded water drops that splattered on the garden's stepping stones; muddy places in the road which I always tried to avoid so as not to dirty my shoes. With a sudden rush, thoughts of home flooded my mind.

Mother set her tray on the heater by the window, and her shoulders slumped as she ate. I wondered if I had ever considered how my parents felt spending this important holiday each year without their eldest son in attendance. I wanted to apologize to my mother for forcing her like this to spend one of my uncommon New Year's Days with me.

March 1971

It was during my ninth month in the hospital that I left my room for the first time. I was going to the outpatient clinic to have my neck X-rayed. I was told that they could do it in my room, but the bones in my neck were now firmly in place, and as my doctor said, "It's time you had a change of scenery."

With my neck carefully secured, I was cautiously moved onto a gurney. As we set off down the hallway, my mother pulled from in front, giving me a cheerful guided tour.

"This is the assistant professor's office. This is the washroom. Remember 'S' who came to visit so often? This was his room."

We stopped and looked in at the nurses' station. The nurses looked much more serious as they moved about busily there than they did when they came to my room. In front of the nurses' station was the ice machine. I was surprised at how far away it was from my room. Was this how far Mom came to get ice in the middle of the night? Whenever she took a long time getting back, I imagined that she had stopped along the way to talk with someone. Now I realized, guiltily, how wrong I had been. Surely she had run through the halls as fast as she could.

Cherry trees were blooming in a little courtyard. Nurse Kamimura stopped the gurney by a window to show me. Four or five years later, I told her how thrilled I had been.

"I was glad to be alive. Looking at such a beautiful sight, I realized how wonderful life is."

At that time, however, I was unable to utter a word.

I waited outside the X-ray room while mine were being developed. The toilet was right next-door, and people were constantly going in and out. Whenever anyone opened the door, the smell wafted out. I was moved by that nostalgic odor, even though I knew the smell of a toilet is a strange thing to get excited about. It should have been repulsive. When I thought about it, though, I had breathed that particular smell every single day of my life—until my accident almost ten months ago. My injury had even meant separation from this. Actually, I had forgot all about it. The toilets at home, at my elementary school, at my college dorm, and at Kuragano Junior High.

I wasn't sure why, but from somewhere inside of me an emotion surged:

I'm alive. My life will continue!

April 1971

In the courtyard garden outside my window, the double-blossom cherry trees were finally in bloom. Beautiful flowers took over each branch, bowing them under their weight. A number of patients in brightly-colored pajamas stood under the trees viewing the blossoms. The scene was lovely enough to be in a movie: people whose heads were wrapped in bandages, people on crutches or in wheelchairs, pregnant women from the maternity ward. Then there were all the patients who could not leave their rooms, all with their own thoughts, who must certainly have been looking from their windows at those cherry trees.

Mr. Mogi, an older man who had been a newspaper reporter in his younger years, wrote short poems on strips of writing paper as he looked at the blossoms, then read them aloud to the others in our room.

While still a teenager Mr. Mogi had got osteomyelitis in one leg, but he persevered, dragging his foot behind him, and went to work for a local newspaper. When older, he had even started a small newspaper of his own.

Recently, his leg had gotten worse until it had become a matter of life or death, so he had finally decided to have it amputated. He often told us he was glad to be parting with the source of his pain of sixty years, but also that he felt sadder and sadder as the surgery date drew closer.

Mr. Mogi poured that sadness into his poems. Later, the pain after the amputation and the struggle of having only one leg went into them, too.

> Watching a thin line of blood
> Flowing silently through the transfusion tube
> I think of life

He often shared with us the romance and adventures of his reporting career. He was always cheerful and, to me, heroic.

I had a feeling that it was more than his past exploits that gave this old man his firm grip on life. Mr. Mogi moaned and groaned and fully admitted how much it hurt. Sometimes he made a show of false bravery. But then he would put it all into his poems. It was as if he were playing with his pain.

> In the pre-dawn quiet comes my favorite nurse
> to take my pulse
> Never shall I forget those icy fingers

It was his ability to put his feelings into poems that kept this 80-year-old man with only one leg far more alive and sprightly than the rest of us.

Here I was, capable of saying nothing more than "it hurts" when in pain, nothing better to say than "lovely" when looking at the cherry trees.

May 1971

One of our roommates, Mr. Tanaka, had been transferred to a private room just before his surgery. About ten days after it was over, his wife came to our room with a tape recorder.

"My husband wants to hear your voices," she said. Mr. Tanaka, a father of two, had a bone disease that had necessitated the amputation of one leg at his buttocks.

We all recorded our thoughts and words of encouragement. Mr. Mogi, in usual form, recited a poem written by Takuboku, a famous modern Japanese poet.

Putting on airs, I gave my rendition of Tatsuji Miyoshi's poem "On a Temple Path." Mr. Tanaka was now in the same private room that I had occupied. I knew that he was lying there, staring at the same ceiling. I wanted him to hear the same poem that had calmed my heart with its soothing words.

On the farthest side of our room was a junior-high student whom everyone called "Tabo." His mother held the mike up to him,

"Come on, Tabo, why don't you say something?"

She was from the Tohoku district and had a gentle accent. Tabo was shy and refused to say a word.

"Anything's fine, Tabo. Come now, say something, there's a good boy."

When we listened to the tape later, this one-sided exchange had a very pleasant effect. Maybe Tabo's mother had assumed that since Tabo was the one who had been asked to speak, her voice would not be recorded; at any rate, the voice of a mother speaking gently to her child wrapped me as warmly as my mother's arms had done, long ago. Even before Tabo's mother's voice reached Mr. Tanaka, it had consoled all of us. It even seemed to comfort Mr. Mogi and the other attending mothers. My mother, my mother's mother. The kindness of a mother is something understood by anyone, anywhere, anytime.

That winter, Tabo had taken a fall while skiing and had been paralyzed in the same way as I was. When he first came to us from another hospital, he had been continuously downcast, hardly talking at all. Lately, however, he had begun joining in our conversations. When we finally got to know him, we found out that he was a normal kid, full of fun and mischief.

Why did something so tragic have to happen to such a blameless child? I was more indignant over him than for myself and prayed fervently for his recovery.

I've just about accepted my own fate, but please do something for that boy.

Then, one day, Tabo's arm moved a little. At first he felt a tingling and then pain when his mother washed him down. Then the pain turned into feeling, and his legs began to move just a little. One day someone stood him up beside his bed, and his knees began to act like a spring, making his legs bounce up and down. His worried mother tried to keep him down.

"You must be still."

"I can't help it, they're moving!" Tabo exclaimed joyfully.

"That's great, Tabo. That's really terrific."

All the people in our room and those visiting from other rooms congratulated him.

Control of his bodily functions returned, and he was soon able to feed himself. Tabo was a new person, filling our whole room with laughter and his boyish humor.

Thanks to Tabo, even I began to tell strings of jokes and puns. I remembered how much I had always enjoyed making people laugh. Tabo thought of me as his elder brother; whenever anyone brought either of us something to eat, we always shared it.

Even so, I could not ignore the horrible feeling that was taking root inside me. I hated to admit it, but I was jealous of Tabo. I had prayed so hard for his recovery, yet, when it miraculously happened, a faint shadow covered my feeling for him.

Rejoice in his recovery! Rejoice without bitterness! You're not that mean! I screamed at myself. I must have been born with a sad heart. When people around me have misfortune, I think I am happy. When others have a bit of good luck, then I am sad. Can there be any true happiness—one that does not depend on looking right or left at other people all the time? Can I not be happy at the same time other people are? It would not have to be any big thing. If I could only be truly happy over Tabo's recovery, I would look so much more cheerful!

>Putting down roots in black soil
>Drinking muddy water
>How can you bloom so beautifully?
>Surrounded by the love of so many
>Why do I have only ugly thoughts?
>
>(Japanese Iris)

In June, my lungs were back to normal and my breathing was stable, so the doctors closed up the hole in my throat. My mother was thrilled that she could finally go out for a meal and take her time without having to worry every minute. For an entire year while the hole had been in my windpipe, phlegm was always in the way, making it necessary for me to be within easy reach of the suction machine, day and night.

Once the tube was removed from my throat, the surrounding flesh closed in over it, making the hole much smaller, but as long as it was there, it was a source of worry.

Now that no air leaked from my throat, I was able to speak in a much louder voice.

July 1971

With my mother pushing me on a gurney, I went out

into the hallway. Every time we passed someone going the opposite direction, I could feel their eyes on me. Despite this, it was fun going back and forth along the main hallway, watching people clad in various colors as they passed by. I was lying down as always—but at least my body was in motion, and it proved a needed relief from the same old ceiling and window I spent every day gazing at.

Near the entryway my mother stopped the gurney, and while we were looking outside a middle-aged man came over and began to talk with us. He had been in the hospital until recently and now came back occasionally as an outpatient. He asked me about my illness. I did not want to say that I was completely unable to move, so I gave a vague answer. From my attitude he must have thought I was despondent over my illness, because he tried to cheer me up by telling me, in a gentle voice, the story of a certain young man.

This young man had fallen from an exercise bar. His arms and legs were paralyzed, and he had been bedridden now for several years. He managed to eat with someone feeding him, but as for the other end the man was not sure. All day, every day, all he did was stare at the ceiling and do nothing. He was merely living—nothing more.

While I was listening to the story, astonished that there could be someone else like me, the man mentioned that this young man had also been a P.E. teacher. Not only that, he had been injured soon after graduating from college, and he was still in that very hospital.

"Now that's a pitiful person," the man said. "You're still young, you don't know how much luckier you are than he is. Now cheer up, and get better."

I couldn't look at his face. Except that the young man had fallen from a bar, everything else meshed with my experience. Maybe he really is talking about me.... Suddenly I was enveloped in desolation.

"What ward is that man in?"

My voice must have sounded near tears.

"I hear he's in orthopedics. Poor guy. Even modern medicine can't cure him, they say."

I asked my mother to get me out of there quickly. My face must have gone pale. The man might have realized what he had done, because I thought I heard him take five or six steps after us.

So that's how other people look at me, I thought. What that man said was true.

Even now, people who came to see me said, "You're looking good," or "You'll be up and about in no time."

They weren't telling the truth. These were lies told out of kindness.

"He's merely living—nothing more."

That man's words kept ringing in my ears. Was I going to finish my life as he said, staring vacantly at the ceiling? Each breath brought a new wave of desolation. I wondered if my mother, pushing me along, was feeling the same....

August 1971

One of the medical-school professors had told me that people with cervical spinal cord damage have to be careful during summer, and it was true. After the rainy season, when the heat set in, I could hardly eat at all. Despite the lack of sensation below my neck, it felt as if my body were cooking on a grill.

"I feel like I'm wearing boots filled with boiling water," I complained to the doctor. The worst part of it was, if someone put ice to my body I could not feel the coolness. My temperature rose to 38 °C and refused to go down.

The doctor explained that it was because I could not sweat. With my kind of injury, even the sweat glands are paralyzed. I found that hard to believe, so the doctor used a hand mirror to show me my body. Sure enough, even though it was hot, there was not a drop of sweat on my legs or stomach. In fact, I looked positively dried up.

The doctor told me, "Keep your body cooled down with ice and drink lots of water to get rid of your fever by urination, and ...."

I opened my mouth and stuck out my tongue,

"Heh, heh, heh," I panted.

My mother opened her eyes wide in surprise.

"Like a dog!" I laughed, "I'll get rid of the heat by sticking out my tongue!"

But my body! I was shocked at what the mirror had revealed. It would not suffice to say that I had lost weight. It was as if skin had been painted over my bones. My chest looked like a washing board, and my pelvic bones looked as though they had been pushed right through my skin. My legs resembled two thin branches on a paulownia tree. I reminded myself of a picture that I had seen of prisoners in the concentration camp at Auschwitz. This was the first look I had of my horribly transformed body.

October 1971

The *keyaki* trees in the hospital courtyard had taken on some color. It was autumn again.

I often saw a young girl looking out of a fifth-story window of the building opposite mine. I could not see her face but recognized her by the sky-blue bathrobe she always wore. Twice a day, in the morning and at sunset, she would gaze out the window for about half an hour. Her room faced north, so she could probably see the great base of Mt. Akagi as well as Mt. Haruna, and maybe even the already snow-covered peaks of the Joetsu mountain range. Above her was a breathtaking blue sky. For me it was the long-awaited autumn sky which had finally come after a burning hot summer. As I lay looking up at that sky day after day, I imagined I could feel myself gradually being dyed the same color.

One day as I was looking at the girl in the blue gown, I suddenly got the feeling that she was watching me; and the more I watched her, the more it seemed she was looking my way. Her room was on the fifth floor. My small ward had the base of the three Jomo mountains as a backdrop, and my room was on the first floor, sunken slightly below ground level and partially hidden from view. There was no reason for her eyes to find me. Still, it seemed that our feelings had collided with each other so squarely that I felt a little bashful.

One day when the sky was a particularly spectacular blue, I escaped from my room, and, pushed on the gurney, visited the fifth floor of her building. Whether she was always looking at the mountains or at the sky above it, I was not sure, but I wanted to see whatever it was, too. Lying down I might not be able to, but any little part of it would be fine. I had to have a look.

The fifth floor housed the neurosurgery ward. There were rooms on both sides of the hallway, so I did not know where to look out at the scenery, nor did I know which room was hers. But Mother and I went boldly down the hallway, opened an emergency exit, and found that it led to another hallway connecting the ward with a research section. On both sides of this hallway were square windows with rounded corners. Strikingly framed in the windows were the blue sky, brilliant white clouds, and Mt. Akagi, already taking on the red colors of fall.

About ten minutes later a girl in a sky-blue gown passed by us. She stopped to gaze at the mountain from a spot about two windows away from us. Recognizing her hair style and the profile of her face, I was certain that it was my fifth-floor-window girl. As she looked out, she occasionally glanced over at me, so I finally had my mother push me over to her, and asked outright.

"You always look out of the window from here, don't you?"

Her face suddenly lit up.

"You're the man from orthopedics, right? Can you see me from your room?"

"How could I help watching such a pretty lady every day?"

"When you came down my hallway a few minutes ago, a person in my room said, 'That man from orthopedics who never gets out of bed just headed toward the connecting hallway!' I had to finish taking my temperature, then I came to get a close-up look at you."

"Can you really see me so well from your room?" I asked.

"You don't move at all, do you? My roommates and I have often wondered what your illness is."

"Wow! If you can see that much, you must be able to see—everything!" I said wrinkling up my nose.

At first glance she did not seem to have anything wrong with her. I learned that she had been in an automobile accident and was in the hospital to take detailed tests to check for aftereffects.

As we talked, I discovered that "Miss K" was the same age as I. From that day on she came to my room almost every day and helped cheer all of us up. I was delighted by how honest I could be with her. Healthy people always tried to encourage me with words such as "youth," "patience," and "tenacity," but Miss K never used them once. Neither did I feel pity from her. We just enjoyed talking together.

One night from a fifth-floor window, she used a flashlight to make characters and send me a message.

Good night. See you tomorrow.

I asked my mother to send a similar message for me.

Good night. Get to bed, kid.

She replied in big characters,

Shut up and go to sleep yourself.

After that we had flashlight conversations every evening.

Fall ended, and winter set in. Every night Miss K sent me messages. Once, however, my mother was away and I could not reply. She watched my room for a while and began writing again.

I'm leaving here tomorrow, and then in smaller strokes, *I love you.*

Just before lights out, she appeared in my room and spoke quietly into my ear,

"Did you see what I wrote?"

"Sure, I saw it," I tried to sound offhand.

"I'm transferring to Sawatari Hospital. I'll come visit."

She sounded sad. After she left, she wrote me often. From Sawatari Hospital, located in the mountains, she sent me red leaves from Japanese maples and little berries folded into her stationary. She also sent me poems. When she was finally able to go home, she wrote about her first visit to a *pachinko* parlor and her first time back at church. At the end of the letter she wrote two or three verses of *tanka* (short poems) of the sort she had written since she was a child. Miss K used no fancy words; her poems were clear reflections of her artless, unpretentious character. Miss K taught me something important: do not pretend to be what you are not. She taught me the beauty of living bravely and proudly just as one is.

February 1972

It began snowing one afternoon. Whenever it snows I have a great desire to go out and play like a child. Even though it was cold, I pestered my mother into taking me out into the hallway. In the now-deserted outpatient section, there was a big window, and my mother lined me up against it so that I could watch the falling snow.

Cold air came through the chinks between the windows, so Mother pulled my quilt all the way up to my eyes. Watching the endless gray snow falling from the white sky, I began to feel as if I were floating through the sky on a magic carpet.

After we returned to my room, my mother's fears were soon realized. I had taken in too much cold air, and as soon as I was back in bed, phlegm began to build up in my throat. Just as the branches of trees outside became heavier and heavier with snow, the blockage in my throat built up until it was difficult to breathe. The nurse came and put the tube to the respirator into my mouth because the hole from the tracheotomy was closed, but breathing did not get any easier.

My chest muscles were paralyzed so that I could only breathe abdominally. I could neither breathe deeply nor clear my throat at all. The doctor on duty tried putting me on my side, slapping me on the back, and all manner of things, but I still felt as though I were drawing breath through a pinhole.

A nurse yelled for Dr. Nishimura, who was passing by on his way home. He rushed in, but I did not have enough air to tell him how painful it was, so to convince him I drew on what little strength I had and shook my head back and forth.

When he ordered me to open my mouth, it sounded as distorted as if he was talking underwater, and his face, as it drew closer to mine, was blurry. Dr. Nishimura blew his own breath into my lungs over and over, until my vision came back into focus and I could hear clearly again. With each breath, more than just air, his gentleness and strength filled my chest in a way mere oxygen never could have.

The next day, another tracheotomy was performed. To make sure the hole did not close, a tube was inserted and securely attached. It was to be left open until there was no longer any danger of my throat being blocked.

CHAPTER FOUR

I Want To Write

March 1972 to May 1973

(Rose)

From the Doctor's Report

Most of the patient's bodily functions, breathing, and temperature have stabilized. The hole from the tracheotomy was left open so that the respirator can be used if he should have further difficulty breathing. There is no indication that his paralysis will be cured, nor is there any treatment available in modern medicine. Total care of his bodily functions is the only recommendation.

From Mother's Reminiscences

I was so downhearted after the second tracheotomy. Just when it seemed that things were settling down, we had to go back all the way to the beginning. I do not know how many times I wished that I could go to sleep and not have to wake up to a new day. Then I would think about what would become of Tomihiro if anything should happen to me and knew I could not complain. I knew that I had to stay with him for the rest of my life, do anything that would make him happy. That has been my will since the beginning.

He continued to run a fever, and his stomach swelled. There was no hope that things would get better; all we could do was to wait as long as it took for his strength to return. Tomihiro too must have been thinking about the future. I was surprised at how much time he spent just staring at the ceiling. I could not think of any words to soothe him. He read everyday—all of Eiji Yoshikawa's books and many others. I put in a device to hold the books and turned each page for him. He read as if trying to absorb each character, each word.

He was bolstered by letters from friends and students, and I knew how badly he wanted to write replies. But he did not have the strength in his neck to lift his own head, let alone do anything else.

March 1972

My second spring in the hospital. As the sunlight coming through the window bathed me in its gentle rays, I was slowly recovering. All the expressions of spring—the lengthening of days, the increasing warmth—brought hope to those of us confined to our beds. Even I began to feel livelier, and I enjoyed making people laugh with my puns and jokes, just as I had done when I was a student.

One day in a conversation with a nurses' aid, I joked,

"Ah...I want a girl! Old woman, I want a young damsel!"

"I see, Young Master. What sort of damsel would be your pleasure?"

"About seventeen or eighteen years old—but no, I shan't be particular. Even one who is a bit misshapen, as you yourself were in your younger years, would be fine."

"The Young Master's wish shall be fulfilled. I shall certainly find you a fetching damsel."

A few days later, about two o'clock in the afternoon, a middle-aged woman from the private room across the hall brought me some peach blossoms.

"A girl from Room 2 or 3 brought these, but I don't know her. When I asked the nurses' aid, she said they must have been meant for Mr. Hoshino, so I brought them here."

As soon as the woman left, a long-haired girl with a cast on her leg appeared in front of me, carefully holding more peach blossoms.

She smiled and said, "Mr. Hoshino? My name is Annaka. I heard about you from the nurses' aid. I wanted to come sooner, but I couldn't before today."

The nurses' aid must have gone to the women's room and told them all my "young damsel" story!

Miss Annaka was a test analyst at the hospital who had broken her leg on a ski trip, and she had just begun to walk again. From that day on she often came by to see me. When she found out that I liked to read, she brought me a book entitled *Shiokari Pass*.

The train that connects the towns of Teshio and Ishikari in Hokkaido goes through a mountain pass called Shiokari. Many years ago, there was an accident on that pass in which the connector between two train cars broke, and the rear car began to roll backwards down the slope. The hand brake would not work, so a young railman threw his own body underneath the wheels of the train, stopping it and thereby saving many lives. *Shiokari Pass* was the retelling in novel form of this true story. As I read the book I recalled the number of times I had been saved from death, including the time Dr. Nishimura gave me mouth-to-mouth resuscitation. I was deeply impressed by the spirit of the young railman, and by the depth of his love.

Miss Annaka also lent me two other books by the same author, Ayako Miura. Until that time I had only heard the name, but I soon learned that she had spent thirteen bedridden years doing nothing but staring upwards. As I read, I was moved by each word. Gradually, the words found their way into the depths of my feelings, to the dark, hidden recesses where all my grief was stored, and thrust in a ray of light. For example, Mrs. Miura wrote:

"To live is not a privilege, but a duty."

"We are not merely alive: we are given life."

At every point in her books she included Bible verses and impressive examples of people called Christians who lived according to them.

Actually, I had a Bible. It was in a cardboard box under my bed. I felt that letting other people know I even had a Bible would reveal just how weak I was, so I had put it away under my bed without ever opening it once. After I read a second book by Ayako Miura, I asked my mother to put the Bible on a little bookshelf I kept beside my bed. It had been Tabo's bookshelf, and he gave it to me when he was transferred from Gundai to another hospital for rehabilitation.

Now that I had the Bible out, I spent a number of days staring sidelong at the characters on its cover.

A friend named Yoneya, who was two years older than I and had been in my college dormitory, had brought it to me. At about that time, as I spent each day looking up from my bed at the spring sky, I had begun imagining myself ten years from then lying in the same bed in exactly the same position. This discouraging prospect had led me into the habit of biting my tongue. Since I could not move my arms or legs, I had tried a few times to bite through my tongue. Not having the courage to do so, I settled for a sad little habit whereby I amused myself by flirting with death.

Then Yoneya came to visit me. Once, during college, when he was making instant *ramen* noodles at the dormitory, I gave him a cabbage leaf to add to it, and in turn he gave me half of his noodles. At the time, I had no money and nothing to fill my stomach with besides some old cabbage and figs from our garden, so I was impressed by his kindness and thankful for the *ramen*.

When Yoneya visited me at the hospital, I shared that memory with him. Then I said,

"I could really use some cold Chinese noodles!" This refreshing dish is made only in the summer, and there was no chance of getting it during the cold early spring. But my whole body was hot from the fever that may have been induced by my paralysis, and I really wanted some cold noodles.

"Please let me pray," Yoneya said before he left. I did not want him to, but how could I refuse after he had been so kind as to come so far to see me. Ignoring my confusion, Yoneya put his hand on my forehead and began to pray.

"Oh Lord...."

I opened my eyes a tiny bit and looked around the

room. I was afraid the others in my room would think I
had called him in to perform some hocus-pocus to cure
me. I did not have the faintest idea then how Yoneya's
prayer was going to change the rest of my life. Instead, I
myself prayed underneath his big hand,

Yoneya, please lower your voice!

About an hour after he had left, as I was thinking what
a terrific friend he would be if he did not have to mention
Christ so often, he showed up again. Wrapped up in the
cloth he carried was a bowl of cold noodles!

I enthusiastically dug in. There must be more to this
Christ than meets the eye! I thought. The noodles felt
good inside my feverish body, but after eating nothing but
rice gruel for so long, I could not eat even half of Yoneya's
present. I was disappointed in myself. I was sure that
eating only half would be only half an expression of
gratitude.

As I watched Yoneya leave, I thought wretchedly about
how he had been as considerate of me as if he himself
were ill; and how I, full of nobody else's pain but my
own, had given up on life. It was not long after this that
he gave me the Bible.

Almost every night I heard a woman somewhere crying.
Sometimes she sobbed, and sometimes she wailed
hysterically. Through the grapevine of people who
attended to their hospitalized relatives, I heard that the

voice belonged to a young girl in a private room whose leg had been amputated.

"They say she was even engaged to marry...." was the rumor that came around. When I heard the weeping begin I would be drenched in sadness. I could not sleep a wink all night. This continued for several days in a row, and then stopped completely one night. The next day a woman who introduced herself as the girl's mother brought me a letter. The girl herself, whose name was Ogiwara, had written it. It was hard to believe that the same person who had done all that crying had filled several pages of stationary with such beautiful handwriting.

> I heard about you from a nurse. I'm ashamed of myself for thinking I was the one in the most pain and with the worst luck. I won't cry anymore. I'll think of you being so cheerful and try to do better myself.

I didn't think I was quite as bright and cheery as Miss Ogiwara pictured me. I was delighted, however, to know that just as I was, I could be useful to someone. Someday, when she was well enough to walk, Miss Ogiwara would come to see me. I decided that I had better do my best to become thoroughly good-humored so that she would not be disappointed. I wanted to be like Ayako Miura and others who were able to work even though they could not move. I decided that the first thing I could do in that direction was to smile.

Reverend Funaki, the pastor of the church that Yoneya

and Miss Annaka attended, came to see me. Through Mrs. Miura's books and visits from my two Christian friends, I had taken an interest in Christianity, so I was pleasantly surprised by the minister's visit. Still, it was the same as with the others; I winced whenever he mentioned God or Christ, and checked my roommates to see how they reacted. As I inclined my ear to the minister's words, I was thinking of the excuses I would make after he left:

"It's not as though I asked him to come, but, you know, reading the Bible is a good way to study history...."

I was deeply disappointed in myself. Even though I had become painfully aware of my frailty, I still could not admit it to others. Especially now that I was gaining a reputation as being cheerful and someone who refused to give in to a tough situation, I hid my weakness more carefully than ever.

"I want to study the Bible. Please come again," I finally said to Reverend Funaki. These words came from a small tear in the mantle covering my weakness and expressed my true feelings.

The minister came the next week and every week after that. I continued, however, to worry about the people around me and could only take sidelong glances at the Bible on my bookshelf. Then one day, Reverend Funaki picked up my Bible and inserted a bookmark at a certain spot.

"Why don't you start reading here?" he said.

After he left, feeling like a soldier who has finally decided to break into the enemy camp, I had Mother set the Bible in my book-holder. This holder was fixed over my head so that I could lie on my back and read, with my mother turning each page. Anyone else in the room could see exactly what book I was reading. The minister had put the bookmark in at Paul's Letter to the Romans. Even though I found several quotations that Ayako Miura had included in her books, to tell the truth, my great expectations were betrayed by the dry, uninteresting lines of characters that filled the book. Still, I had my mother turn the pages until I came across some words that held my eyes.

> Not only that, but suffering is joy. Suffering produces endurance, endurance brings God's approval, and His approval creates hope....

Yoneya had once sent me a postcard with those words on it, but I had not paid them much attention. Now as I scrutinized them amidst the other, uninspiring lines, I could feel a soft ray of light piercing the shell of my drab future. Even if I couldn't believe the words, I wanted to believe them. I wanted to believe that my present anguish would not end merely as such, but lead to my growth as a human being, and to hope. These words gave me hope.

I recalled an experience, one that probably occurred during my high-school days. I was at home, so it might have been a Sunday. I went to the pigsty, filled a basket with manure, hoisted it onto my back, and headed out to our family field. The heat of the day combined with the moist heat of the manure went straight through the basket into my body. After climbing a short way, I was drenched with sweat. Our field was on the slope of a mountain, so carrying fertilizer and other tasks all had to be done by hand.

Our little village was made up of small houses scattered along the railway running to Ashio City and along the highway leading to Nikko. I heard that during my father's youth, when the Ashio copper mines were at peak production, the village streets bustled with the comings and goings of wagons hauling copper.

In our area there are quite a few places which have the word "flat" as part of the name. The reason is that there are steep mountains everywhere, so the early villagers prized any ground that was not on an incline. Even the tiniest patch of level land still boasts the Chinese character for "flat."

Our field was terraced, and the crops never seemed to live up to the amount of perspiration we invested in them. That day, as always, I climbed up the narrow path that was so steep my nose almost touched the dirt in front of me. Suddenly I came across a small white cross. It was a little grave. The cross had just been placed there, and there was a bouquet of flowers on the mound of freshly dug earth. In small characters on the front of the cross were the words,

> Come to me, all of you who are tired from carrying heavy loads.

Looking back I realized that this was my first contact with the Bible. I read it out loud. The words touched something inside of me, and it might have been because I was a "tired" person covered with sweat who was "carrying heavy loads" of warm pig manure.

But what, I wondered, did "come to me" mean? This question had remained in my mind the whole time I worked in the field that day. And now, as I lay there in bed, it struck me anew with full force.

Summer 1972

Takaku's mother came by to see us some time after he had been transferred to a hospital in Tokyo. Takaku was a junior-high student who had been the pet of everyone in our hospital room, but in Tokyo he was lonely among people he did not know. He had asked his mother to have us record our voices on a cassette tape and to write something on a canvas hat he always kept with him. We enthusiastically gave some raucous renditions of our favorite songs, but when it came to writing I was at a loss.

Takaku's illness was life threatening, and the nurses and

other patients were all eager to write something
encouraging. Finally, the hat came around to me. I was
completely frustrated, but there was nothing I could do—
oh, how I wanted to write! I wanted to be able to move
something. We had been such close friends. I thought
how thrilled Takaku would be to find somewhere on that
hat something that I had written by myself! It would be a
small word of encouragement from one sick person to
another. That did it. I wanted to give Takaku a surprise,
something to make him smile. But how to do it? I hastily
asked my mother to place a pen in my mouth.

This was my first such attempt, and after giving me the
pen, my mother gingerly held Takaku's cap over my face.
I put every ounce of my strength into my neck and lifted
my head. The pen just grazed the cap and made a black
spot about the size of a sesame seed. All I needed to do
was to push the pen, to stretch that spot into a line to
make a character; but making that single, tiny dot was my
limit. I used up every bit of power I had to raise my head.
I was as out of breath as I might have been after running a
race; and I had bitten down on the pen so hard that I had
nearly lost the feeling in my front teeth. Saliva ran out of
my numb lips. It had been a reckless act to try to raise my
head. Finally, my mother pressed the hat down on my
pen and moved the hat back and forth to make the first
character in my name, "Tomi" (富). She cleverly
converted the first black spot into the character "o" (お).
Without moving my neck I had managed to write "O-

Tomi," acquiring thereby the name of a legendary and adventurous *geisha*.

A few days later we got a call from Takaku. He had been delighted with my "O-Tomi" signature, and we chatted together for more than half an hour. He was so happy that I could not bear to tell him that I had done no more than hold the pen in my mouth.

As I listened to his voice I was overjoyed to know how excited he was, and at the same time I was filled with a fierce desire: *I want to write!*

I had received lots of letters since I had entered the hospital. Most of the students I had taught were now in high school. Even though I had taught them for only two months, they still called me *sensei*. They told me in great detail about their new high schools, friends, athletic events, trips, home life and so forth. They wrote things such as, "I'm writing this during class...," and "Today I'll tell you about my boyfriend. You're the only one who knows, so don't tell anyone." Some corresponded with me for almost two years.

My mountain-climbing friends and the nursing students who came for training also sent letters. Nothing cheers up someone confined to a sick room so much as a letter from the outside. I read each one again and again, then faced each letter and silently thanked its writer. Over and over, I thought of how much it would mean to those who wrote, as well as to myself, if I could send even a short reply. I had no proof that I might be able to do it, but nonetheless I asked my mother to buy me a sketchbook and a felt-tipped pen. I thought that the sturdy paper in a sketchbook would be easier for her to hold. The sketchbook, however, was left for months without a line, let alone a single character, being written on it.

When I had lifted my head, it had felt like I had raised it a good distance; but it had been no more than two or three millimeters. I felt as though I would need the strength to lift a weight of several hundred kilograms in order to actually move it any further. But I did not want to give up. Giving up writing with a pen in my mouth would be more than just abandoning my only wish; I felt that it would be giving up on life.

> On the contrary, we cannot do without the parts of the body that seem to be weaker. (I Corinthians 12:22)

These were words that I found as I read the Bible.

If there really were a God, as the Bible claimed, then that God surely cared about people like me. And he would give me work to do. I thought my work at that point might be to write with a pen in my mouth, and I fervently hoped that there was a God.

December 1972

Even though my room was inhabited by patients with serious illnesses, it was, with the exception of surgery days, a lively place. We especially looked forward to nursing students who came for training periods, because they filled our room with youthful energy.

Miss Shinohara was the student nurse assigned to me that December. She was reserved but became a picture of intensity as she fed or washed me down. Despite the winter cold, perspiration glistened on her forehead.

"Please let me know anything I can do for you," she told my mother and me.

To prevent bedsores, I was turned on my side two or three times a day. So that I would not topple over, quilts were rolled up and placed on either side of me. Then on top of all that, a long sash was wrapped around me and the whole bed to hold me in place.

I decided to waste no time in asking a favor of Miss Shinohara.

"Miss Shinohara, excuse me, but would you mind taking the place of these rolled-up quilts?"

"What? I didn't expect to hear anything like that from you."

I had disconcerted her, but she was able to answer back. The others in the room joined in.

"Miss, this would be a great favor to Mr. Hoshino. Please take the place of those quilts!" They only encouraged me.

"Miss Shinohara, why do you look so embarrassed? Did you actually think...? No! I was merely thinking in medical terms. Now, please consider, to a patient unable to move, which would have more of a therapeutic effect, rolled-up quilts or a young girl? Let me assure you, I'm quite serious."

"I'm sure it wouldn't help you mentally, and it would certainly be bad for your heart." Even as we joked, Miss Shinohara was thinking carefully about what I might actually be able to do in that position.

A few days later, when I was turned on my side, she said,

"Why don't you try writing in this position?" Every once in a while, someone says something that can change the course of a person's life.

Once I had mentioned the same thing to my mother, but I had never seriously considered any position except facing up, and so a good idea had been shoved off to a corner. I once heard a story about the Mayan Indians who had made toys with wheels for their children but never realized that the wheels could be used as a means of transportation. That story reminded me of myself.

While I was still turned on my side, Miss Shinohara held my sketchbook in front of my face. I took the pen, wrapped in gauze, in my mouth. She positioned the paper so that it almost touched the pen. I thrust my neck out slightly and made a black mark on the paper. Since I did not have to move my head off the pillow, it did not take much effort at all. What should I write first? Well, I could not afford to remain idle, but all the words and characters I had thought of completely disappeared from my head.

What I finally wrote was a big "a" (ア), the first

character in the Japanese syllabary. Then I wrote an "i" (イ), which is the next character. Characters that looked like pieces of tangled-up black thread started filling up the page. I became dizzy. The gauze around the pen was soaked in saliva which trailed down my cheek and onto my pillow. Having this unfamiliar object in my mouth also made me feel nauseous. But I was so excited, I couldn't stop!

Miss Shinohara's hands began to tremble as she held the sketchbook. My mother, peering over at me, had her teeth clenched as hard as I did. My neck got tired, and my writing became no more than a scribble, but I still could not stop. I was as exhilarated as I had been as a child the first time I had been able to write my own name.

That night I broke out in a high fever. But I could not wait for the next day when I would write again. Tomorrow, I decided, I would try to write more slowly and calmly. For the first time in a long time I had a good, deep night's sleep.

I thought I would like to try some gymnastics. Of course I was not going to use the bar or rings, but I decided to practice the same way I had trained in gymnastics. When somebody first watches a gymnastics performance, they think that only a person with some special ability can do it; but even athletes who win Olympic medals cannot do stunts like the Ultra C without learning a pyramid-like structure of easier, less interesting stunts that lead up to that peak. The most normally-used techniques are ones that anyone can learn with practice. From my first year in high school until my college graduation—no, until the instant of my accident—I had practiced gymnastics. I was not an exceptional athlete by any means; but I had learned most of the techniques for floor exercises, vaulting horse, rings, parallel bars, and exercise bar. The reason one can learn to do things that at first glance seem impossible is to start from the basics and repeat the easy movements over and over again. In order to make my body limber, I had spent days and days doing nothing more than forward and backward rolls on the mat—that was all I could do at first. There was nothing flashy or fun about it, but the result was that little by little I began to master the more difficult techniques that people usually associate with gymnastics.

It must be the same, I reasoned, with writing by mouth. As one could learn fancy gymnastic feats by beginning with the basics, surely one could learn to write beautifully with a pen in his mouth. I didn't care if it took years. As one who had practiced gymnastics and had been injured at it, as a P.E. teacher, I felt it was the task now given to me.

What did it matter if I could not write well or quickly? Had I not been helpless the first time I had hung from the rings?

[Sketchbook] First characters written with a pen held in my mouth. Japanese syllabary: *katakana*

January 1973

I greeted my third new year in the hospital. Because of
the international energy crisis that year, the hospital had
to economize on heating. My mother rested her feet on a
hot-water bottle and tried to endure the cold. We spent a
miserable New Year's Day.

Still, I had learned to write and thus was in good spirits.
It had been less than a month since I had begun practice,
and already the shaky lines had become straighter. My
first characters had been about two inches tall, but now I
could write them much smaller. I had even advanced
from the relatively simple syllabary to the more difficult
Chinese characters *(kanji)*. The time I could spend writing
while lying on my side had increased from ten minutes to
thirty, and sometimes even an hour on good days. I still
drooled a lot and felt queasy, but even that cleared up as I
became used to writing. Sometimes it took me several
minutes to draw just one *kanji,* but being able to write on a
sheet of white paper was much too exhilarating to worry
about that. Every day I copied about three lines of
Sakutaro Hagiwara or Jukichi Yagi's poems. I also wrote
some of my favorite Bible verses.

My mother watched over my progress, literally. She
was not allowed to move while holding the sketchbook;
she even stifled her sneezes. There were many times
when she ran for the restroom the instant I let go of my
pen.

One day, Mt. Asama, a nearby active volcano, exploded and darkened Maebashi's sky with its ash. This abrupt act of nature made me feel as if something new was suddenly going to happen inside of me, too. Full of anticipation, I took my pen and wrote:

> Someone is coming
> Carrying a red flower
> Walking in my direction

When I read this over later I was embarrassed because it sounded like something a teenage girl might come up with, so I threw it away.

But that person really did come, and she carried a bag of mandarin oranges instead of a red flower.

"I'm Masako Watanabe from Maebashi Christian Church. I've heard about you from Reverend Funaki."

Mother was out shopping, so, in her place, this young women fed me an orange and then left. From that day on, she visited me every Saturday. At some point, her visits increased to two and then three times a week. When I had a fever she would stop by the hospital every day on her way home from work. She did not always come to my room; sometimes she would just look towards the light of my window and pray for me.

March 1973

Four months after I began to write, I was able, at long

[Sketchbook]
(upper) Ramdom memos
(lower) Verses copied from the Bible
and favorite poems used to practice
writing: (R) Psalm 3:12 (L)Verses from
Jukichi Yagi's poems "Simple Harp"
and "Eyes"

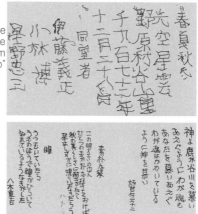

last, to write letters. I wrote to former students, my sisters and friends. It would sometimes take a week to write one letter, but the recipient would be even more overjoyed than I imagined and would send a reply immediately. One friend even framed my letter. Even if I broke out in a fever after writing for a long period of time, I never regretted it. I felt as though these letters that I had written with all my might and soul were extensions of myself. I could not leave the hospital, but my letters would ride a train to some far-off place, taking a part of me with them.

May 1973

I went out to the hospital's back garden on a gurney. It was the opposite of the well-kept front garden. It was full of decayed wooden structures, rubble, and weeds. I, however, prefer overlooked places that have the smell of soil and always went to this back garden on clear, windless days. I would gaze at the sky silently. I never got tired of that sky. I would forget my paralysis and imagine myself swimming freely through eternity.

If I turned my head to one side, I could see some small cottonweed. In Japanese we call this the "mother-and-child" plant. Feeling as if I were floating, drifting in the bright May sky, I was moved by that name.

> When Mother pushed my cart
> Out to the back garden,
> The mother-and-child plant
> Was blooming
> Leaning against a burnt concrete ruin.
> I looked up at the sky, as a flower does
> And the brightness made my eyes tear.
> I was embarrassed
> Lest Mother think I was crying.

(Cottonweed)

On her way to the hospital one day, Miss Watanabe picked for me some starwort flowers that had been blooming beside the road. Since I had had to weed those particularly strong-rooted plants from our field throughout my childhood, I had never felt anything but contempt for them. Here, arranged properly in a vase, they looked more beautiful than I had ever thought such useless, detestable flowers could. With their yellow centers surrounded by thin white petals and unassuming little leaves, I thought them exquisite. I could not be patient just looking at them; I wanted to capture their beauty in my sketchbook. I decided I would not regard my attempt as a drawing; I would just trace the flowers exactly as they were.

I painstakingly drew each thin petal with a black line, making the white space stand out, and the little flower became as big as a sunflower. All the flowers bloomed facing upwards, but the buds, which I thought may have just wilted, were bent downwards. I thought first of drawing them upright to make them look healthier, but on reflection decided they should be drawn just as they were. The finished picture was small, but stronger and more vivid than any I had ever done by hand. Feeling happy about it, I inscribed a few sentences around it and sent it to a friend. Next I drew the cottonweed, then an iris.... Along with my writing, small flowers began to appear regularly in my sketchbook.

One day I came across a newspaper article about the starwort explaining that the buds face downwards. I was glad I had drawn them just as they were. I was ashamed to have even considered trying to improve on nature. Why, even if a flower was wilted or partly eaten by insects, it was still a wonderful bit of nature.

> In the morning light coming through the blinds
> Two buds have split open into six petals
> As I watch the mysterious scene
> Of petals bending backwards
> I feel my idea of drawing the flowers
> Too haughty
> Instead
> I'll ask for the pleasure of drawing them

(Lily)

[Sketchbook] June 17
"Third anniversary of my accident
Wanted to eat good *sushi*
but the *sushi* bar was closed today"

CHAPTER FIVE

From The Depths Of Despair

July 10, 1973 to December 22, 1974

(Spring aster)

From the Doctor's Report

On July10,1973, the patient was transferred to urology to have bladder stones removed. On August 16, he returned to orthopedics. Nurses report that he is refusing to eat, possibly with the idea of starving himself to death. Some method of rehabilitation which would utilize his remaining functions is being sought, but there appears to be none. (He could ride in a wheelchair if he could move even one finger.) But raising his body not only affects his heart and breathing but also brings on a fever whose source is still unknown, so that we hesitate even to move him. Finally, we obtained a reclining wheelchair with a neck support.)

From Mother's Reminiscences

While all his roommates were released or transferred to other hospitals, Tomihiro alone was left behind. Battling an irreversible condition was making both of us more and more depressed. Tomihiro seemed to be tormented by a fury for which he had no outlet, and he lashed out at me more often. As there were other people in the room, we could not argue with each other in loud voices, so twice I left the room to cry by myself.

He began to listen with more interest to the minister who visited frequently and, at last, he became a believer. I was in favor of anything that had the slightest possibility of saving him from his agony, of somehow leading to hope.

The doctors did everything they could. The special wheelchair they found cast light into the darkness we were living in. Indeed, it opened up a new world for us. Riding in the wheelchair, Tomihiro could for the first time in four years go out among other people. Imagine our happiness after giving up hope that such a thing would ever happen! He had no proper clothes for going outdoors, but even this dilemma was a joy. For the time being, I bundled him in blankets up to his neck like a bug in a cocoon. We were even able to attend the medical school's annual festival.

July 10, 1973

I was transferred to the urology ward where I was to have an operation to remove bladder stones. I had difficulty urinating and then a high fever for about ten days. Checking my bladder, the doctors discovered the condition, a common one among bedridden patients. I learned that when a small amount of urine is always left in the bladder, it gradually develops into stones.

In orthopedics I had been an extremely troublesome patient, but both the doctors and nurses there understood my condition because I had been there for so long. I wondered how it would be for me in another ward that was not used to my special problems.

Luckily, a nurse who had always been kind to me took me over to the urology ward. I encouraged myself by thinking that she would understand my helpless feeling and explain the details of my situation to nurses there.

Urology was on the fourth floor, and I was assigned to a room at the farthest end of the hallway. "Which bed would you like?" A nurse waiting there asked me politely. There were three empty beds, and I chose the one by the window. I wanted to be as close as possible to the window to be able to see outside and gaze at the sky.

A little later the nurse came back with paper and pen. She sat beside me and started asking me questions: date of birth, occupation, date of injury, and so on. Her last question was, "Do you believe in any particular religion?"

"Yes. Christianity."

My own words made my heart pound. It was the very first time that I let another person know of my relationship with God. I had not been able to tell even the minister or the people from the church, though they so often visited me in the hospital to talk about the Bible and to pray for me. I had not read more than half of the Bible or ever attended church. How could I dare say I was a Christian? Yet, I could not simply say "None" when asked about my religion.

I did not know where I was headed in life and had nothing to aim towards. Moreover, being transferred to a totally unfamiliar section of the hospital intensified this feeling of uncertainty until it almost overwhelmed me. I longed for something to rely upon. When this feeling was particularly strong, I could sometimes hear a gentle whisper of words floating past my ears like a breeze:

> Come to me, all of you who are tired from carrying heavy loads.

These were the words that I had read on a white cross in the cemetery behind my parents' house—a sentence that had amazingly remained in my memory throughout the years. I had felt God's intentions for me the day I hesitantly opened the Bible and rediscovered it; I realized then that God had given me His word while I was still an active, carefree teenager.

> Come to me, all of you who are tired from carrying heavy loads, and I will give you rest. Take my yoke and put it on you, and learn from me, because I am gentle and humble in spirit; and you will find rest. For the yoke I will give

you is easy, and the load I will put on you is light.
(Matthew 11:28-30)

I wanted to respond to these words of God. I did not
feel qualified to declare myself a Christian, but I wished to
be close to God, who bade me "Come."

"Christianity." The nurse wrote it down as though it
was the most natural thing in the world. I fancied God
responding to me in the same way. I could picture Him
nodding to me—even me—as I said, "I believe in you,"
and writing my name on His heavenly white pad.

My surgery was over in about an hour. The doctors
removed a big stone the size of a thumbnail and three
smaller ones. Though the operation itself was of the
simplest kind, I was consumed by a lack of physical
power and the heat of dog days. I could not speak or even
swallow gruel because the muscles in my jaws were so
painfully taut, and I was kept alive by intravenous
feeding. Besides this, the bedsores on my back got worse,
and I was completely miserable.

There was a nurse who always spoke to me kindly as I
lay unable to eat or drink. One day, she brought me a
small bottle of orange juice.

"We had an extra bottle. It would be a waste to throw it
out. Would you like to drink it?"

I wondered why she had given it to me of all patients,
but in any case I was pleased and managed to drink a

little.

Several days later the nurse came in again, this time with ice cream. I noticed frost on the package—it was no leftover. Then I remembered how cold the orange juice had been and realized that it was not really an "extra" bottle. When my mother put a spoonful of the ice cream into my mouth, I felt more than its cool sweetness inside of me.

August 1973

About the time we had our first autumn wind, I was returned to orthopedics. My appetite had improved, and I knew that my stint in urology had been successful.

But I left the urology ward in low spirits for I could not forget what a doctor there had told my mother and me.

"We have done virtually everything we can for you here. Are you planning to go back to orthopedics? Of course, it's up to you, but you could consider transferring to a hospital closer to your home." The doctor even recommended a hospital specializing in urology.

His words stunned me; I had thought it a matter of course that I would return to orthopedics. Although I knew perfectly well that modern medicine was incapable of curing me, I had still hoped that there was some device which would keep me from being chained to a bed the rest of my life. Someone might invent a machine to help me eat by myself or a special wheelchair that I could use when I regained more strength.... The doctor, however, had advised me to transfer to a local hospital. Perhaps he had talked with the doctors in orthopedics or simply perceived that I would be a nuisance there. I had been in the hospital for over three years even though patients at Gundai usually moved to other hospitals after, at most, one year. My stay had been too long.

My father went to see the hospital recommended by the doctor, but I longed to return to my old spot in orthopedics. I was quite downhearted and was sure that I could feel at ease only in the hands of the doctors and nurses who had saved my life so many times. In orthopedics there were nurses who had often climbed up four flights of emergency stairs to peek in and cheer me up while I was in the urology ward. I wanted to go back to where they were.

August 16

I returned to orthopedics after an absence of one month. Luckily, I was placed in the same room and, several days later, was moved to my old bed by the window. The chief nurse made this arrangement so that I could expose the bedsores on my back to the sun. Perhaps she also hoped to bolster my sagging spirits.

Returning to orthopedics, I made up my mind to stop being completely dependent on others. I had to start living my life more constructively and try to be inventive in using what resources I had. The big decision was made; but I was still nothing but a sordid, smelly, bedridden patient, frequently running a fever and constantly yelling at my mother to bring me a wet compress, an enema, or something else.

By this time, my mother was drained of all strength and could not lift me up by herself. Seeing this, Miss Masaki, a pretty girl of about twenty, began lending her a hand. Miss Masaki had come from Tokyo to attend to her mentally-handicapped elder brother who was in the hospital with a broken thigh bone and staying in my room. She must have spent years helping her brother, and now she never hesitated to clean up my body wastes. The touch of her fingers always conveyed the gentleness of her heart. My favorite time was when she gave me a shave.

At some point, I began hearing people talking in the hallway at night. Time after time, I caught my name being mentioned by them. Sometimes the voices were those of doctors, and sometimes of nurses, but their words were always similar.

"Why did Mr. Hoshino come back? He has little reason to be here. Think of all those people on the waiting list for empty beds. Patients like him are a pain in the neck...."

I heard these voices night after night.

Whenever I heard them, I wished I could plug my ears and just disappear. After I calmed down, though, I realized that the conversation had nothing to do with me, or that what I took to be human voices was merely the sound of the plumbing. I often heard voices even when the hallway was in total silence. This may have been an auditory hallucination, a symptom of neurosis. I was afraid that I was on the verge of a nervous breakdown.

Every night, as I tried to sleep despite those voices in my ears, I would make up my mind to ask my doctor the next morning if I was causing them too much trouble and, if so, to ask that I be transferred to another hospital. The next day, however, my doctor would come on his rounds and speak to me encouragingly. The nurses always chatted with me in gentle tones as they treated my bedsores, and I would realize how unfounded my anxiety was and forget my silly decision of the night before. Nonetheless, when another night fell, I would hear the same voices again.

My mother had been as concerned as I. One day, she finally asked a nurse whom she had become friendly with what the staff thought about my returning to orthopedics. She replied,

"We certainly discussed whether we should move your son to another hospital. But that will be possible only when he is stronger. For the time being, he had better stay here. This is not a private hospital, so we cannot let patients stay here without good reason however strongly they might wish to do so. Mr. Hoshino is now back in his old bed because our ward has accepted him. Don't worry, you should plan to remain here until the doctors say he may be discharged."

Mother told me what the nurse had said. After that, I was never bothered by those imaginary voices again.

Some time later, a doctor lent me a book on mountains because he knew that I liked them. I was grateful. Each character on the page seemed filled with his kindness.

October 1973

"This is Hoshino. Please give me an enema."

Mother had pressed the buzzer on my bed, and I spoke into a microphone connected with the nurses' station. The patient in the next bed chuckled over my apparent lack of embarrassment and repeated what I had said, mimicking my voice. I was given an enema every other day because I could not empty my bowels by myself.

Shortly after, a nurse came in, and lined up behind her were five or six student nurses!

Oh no, this is too much, I thought, just too much! Why must these students use *me* as a guinea pig for enema practice?

With no apparent consideration of my feelings, the nurse busied herself at placing partitions around my bed.

"You hardly ever used those partitions before, and you needn't make this occasion so special by using them now," I grumbled in a tiny voice. This pitiful, timid resistance was the most I could manage. I had been a guinea pig several times before, but never with more than one or two students at a time. Never had I been forced to expose my bare backside to the eyes of so many students, all of them 19-year-old girls.

Although I could not move an inch, I was a man in his twenties with a normal amount of self-respect and sensitivity. When I had requested an enema in a loud voice over the microphone, who would have guessed how long it had taken me to acquire this matter-of-fact manner, or that its purpose was to conceal my unallayable embarrassment?

The student nurses peered at my bare bottom with such serious countenances. I wondered, bitterly, what they were really thinking.

An orange rubber tube had to be inserted into my anus, and I could see that the nurse was lifting my leg so that the students could get a better look. I closed my eyes. I wanted to plug my ears and cover my face, too. If only I could move my hands to do so, I would not have felt so miserable.

This is for the sake of medical science. It is the only way I can repay the people who take care of me.

I tried to reason with myself in vain, for my embarrassment soon turned into uncontrollable bitterness. I wanted to scream at them:

You idiots! Bare your own rear ends and practice on yourselves everyday if it's so much fun!

I was silent, however, and when it was all over and each

student politely thanked me, I involuntarily replied, "Thank *you* very much." When I realized what I was saying, I couldn't help laughing to myself, thinking that my smiling face must look wry.

November 1973

Because my hands remained motionless, Mother fed me each meal. She used a big spoon to pour soup into my mouth while I lay in bed on my back. Hospital meals were served at short intervals—at 8:00 a.m., noon, and 5:00 p.m.—and as I never moved my body, I was scarcely ever hungry. When I had no appetite, eating was reduced to going through the motions of opening my mouth reluctantly for the food. I hated to eat like this, and I would simply stop eating if my mother dropped even the smallest piece of food on my face.

On one of those days when I felt least like eating, Mother's hand trembled, and soup spilled on my face. This trivial incident triggered my pent-up rage, and all of the sudden I exploded. My poor mother was the only person available to vent it at.

I spat a mouthful of rice into her face and yelled, "Damn it! I'm through eating, you old bag!"

Mother began sobbing as she picked up the rice scattered on the floor.

"I'm devoting my life to you, and you call me an old bag...."

"Stop blubbering. Nobody would care if I were dead.

It's your fault for giving birth to me in the first place. Damn it all!"

Wiping her tears, Mother went out of the room to have her own meal, and she did not come back for some time.

Having once exploded, I could not easily stop my anger. Even when Mother finally came back, I continued to throw harsh words at her.

She must have been good and angry, too, because she refused to speak to me.

Then I heard a fly buzzing nearby. It settled on my face, coming back again and again, as if it knew I could not raise my hands. I shook my head in vain. Finally, my mother, still silent, grabbed a fly swatter. *Smack!* It sounded as though she had got it near my feet. A little later, however, another fly appeared, and it too settled on my face. My mother grabbed the swatter again and positioned herself to attack. Then she seemed to think better of it. She transferred the fly swatter to her left hand and raised her right, aiming it at the fly on my face. But instead of bringing it smashing down, she lowered it

[Sketchbook]
Mother pushing me on the gurney

Mother trying to feed me fish. "Say 'Aah!'"

gently and pressed it against my cheek. The fly, of course, flew away unharmed. On my cheek remained the warmth of Mother's moist hand. Her skin was rough, but it felt so soft. The warmth of her affection for me spread from my cheek and gradually permeated my entire body.

Mother must have hated me for swearing at her so rudely, but that resentment was not strong enough for her to allow flies to bother me, nor could she even manage to swat one on my cheek. I had spat a mouthful of rice at her face, and yet she had gently touched mine to chase a fly away.

She is my mother, the very mother who gave birth to me, the only one I would ever know.

I could not live without her.

I had not drawn for quite a while, but I began again that day. I depicted Mother grabbing a swatter in her left hand and raising her right hand to catch the fly on my face.

> Mother's hands
> Are like the chrysanthemum
> Clenched hard
> Yet so soft
> They are like the chrysanthemum

(Chrysanthemum)

Early summer 1974

"Mr. Kobayashi is calling for you. Please go see him when you are on the gurney," a nurse said to me.

Kobayashi, who had been in the bed across from me, was a high-school student who had practiced karate. He had been struck by a sudden pain in the back after returning home from a karate training camp, and was subsequently hospitalized for a serious spinal disease.

Kobayashi impressed me greatly with his honest character and polite manner. I had become jaded by my prolonged stay in the hospital, so I learned a lot from his refreshing youthfulness. As I wanted to absorb as much of his attitude as possible, I flung off my know-everything attitude and talked freely with him about all sorts of things. During our conversations, I did not have to force myself to be open and honest; I found myself naturally become so.

Kobayashi looked happiest when he was telling me about karate. Curious to know how the hand of a man could crack a pile of tiles or a thick block of ice, I listened eagerly to him and enjoyed reading his picture-filled books on karate. He in turn showed interest in my stories about gymnastics and rock-climbing. He came to think of me as an elder brother, and I became equally attached to him.

After major surgery, Kobayashi was advised to move into a private room, but he had insisted on staying in my room and returned to his old bed across from me.

Following the operation, however, his condition grew rapidly worse, and he was forced to move to a private room after all.

In his new room, he asked for my mother.

"I've got permission to have a TV set in my room, but I feel bad about watching it all by myself, especially since Tomihiro can't have one."

Marveling at his gentle character, I asked Mother to convey my response to him.

"Don't worry about me. If you have a TV, I'll go watch it with you."

One day his mother came up to me in the hallway and told me that he would not live much longer. I had tried to prepare myself for this news. I had heard rumors and recognized his condition as similar to that of other patients who had died. But when it was put to me this bluntly, a chilling sadness shot through me. A nurse told me that Kobayashi no longer had the strength to eat and that he had lost his sight, but in his delirium he sometimes called out my name.

I could not bring myself to visit him. I asked my mother to pull the blanket up over my head so that nobody would see the tears pouring from my eyes. Crying alone—that was all I could do then.

There were many times I wanted to die. My craving for life had been so strong right after I had had the accident.

When I could breathe without a respirator, however, and hope for survival was finally creeping into my life, I began to feel like renouncing it all.

I could not move a muscle. I only lay on my back and stared up at the ceiling. I had to have someone put food in at one end and someone else to help get it out at the other. I felt like nothing more than a blocked drainpipe. Did such an existence have any meaning? Even if I should fall in love with a girl, I would not be able to make love to her. This, too, was an agonizing thought that never left my mind.

Maybe I could kill myself if I bit my tongue off, I thought. I even tried to starve myself to death, but could not endure the stinging hunger. The desire for life always welled up whenever there was any danger of death. I thought of having my mother choke me to death, but I could not ask her to be a murderer.

Remembering how Kobayashi clutched a chest expander and lifted dumbbells preparing for the day when he would be healthy again, I was ashamed of the brief period I spent contemplating suicide. Had I ever really thought about death seriously? Certainly I considered it least seriously during those times I thought I wanted to die.

Death is the only assurance given to every soul that has received life. I would have to die sooner or later. When I thought of killing myself, however, I was trying to escape from the fate that God had planned for me. This, I realized, I ought not to be doing. I decided to live my life to the best of my ability until the time came for my true end.

One day I heard a song on the radio sung by a Japanese singer-songwriter entitled "If I Could Live My Life Twice." As I listened to it, I decided I would not take that attitude. How can a person who cannot make the most of his own life here and now expect to do any better a second time?

> A tree cannot move by itself
> From the place allotted to it by God
> It intently spreads its branches
> And strives earnestly
> To reach the height allowed for it to grow
>
> Trees are my friends.

October 1974

One day Mother came back from an errand with a delighted expression on her face. She told me she had seen a brand-new wheelchair in front of the staff office and that the doctors were busily examining it. She guessed that the wheelchair was for me because it had, unlike most, a support for the neck.

Once during the summer I had told my doctor that I wanted to use a wheelchair. I had wondered if a wheelchair with a support for the neck and an extended footrest was available. I needed such a chair because having been bedridden so long, my knees could hardly bend at all, and my neck did not have the strength to support my head. After considering the notion for a few days, the nurses tried attaching a plate to a wooden wheelchair once used in orthopedics. I tried it several times, but after four years of being flat on my back, I would begin losing consciousness if placed in a sitting position. I would be moved into the wheelchair accompanied by a great flurry of activity, only to have to be put back to bed almost immediately.

A special wheelchair would be expensive, and what would happen if it was purchased and I was not able to use it after all? The chief nurse encouraged me by saying that the doctors were looking all over for one that would be just right for me. The anticipation made my body tingle with joy—as if twice as much blood was coursing through my veins. A new strength seemed to have sprung up inside me. From that day on, I gradually extended the time I spent using a wedge to raise the upper half of my body.

The wheelchair Mother had seen was, in fact, for me. It turned out to be an imported item and was perfectly equipped with a neck support and footrest. Moreover, the back of the chair could be lowered by forty-five degrees, which would help prevent me from fainting. It was as if the chair had been custom-built to suit me.

The first time Mother pushed me in the chair along the hallways, I felt that I was the center of everybody's attention. Full of exuberance, I wanted to greet every single person I saw.

"Hello! Did you notice that I'm in a wheelchair today? Excuse me, Ma'am, would you please have a look at this chair? This is the very first time I've ridden it. It's an imported model, you see. Nothing but the best!"

Mother and I went back and forth along the hallway. We also mingled with the crowds in the outpatient clinic. Never had I felt happier during my four years in the hospital.

When able to walk with my own feet, I had always felt sorry to see anyone in a wheelchair. Sometimes I even felt that I had seen something I should not have. What an arrogant, selfish sympathy!

Now I was filled with joy because I was able to ride in a wheelchair and move around. It was the same delight I had felt the first time I rode a bicycle, when I made my first turn on skis, when I learned how to swim, and when I received my first letter from a girl.

People who walked past, casting sidelong glances at me in the hallway, probably could not guess that my heart was bouncing like a rubber ball. They might have pitied me as I had done others when I was still healthy.

What is happiness? What is joy?

I felt I had got a glimpse of both. They can exist in any

circumstance, however desperate. Joy is not diminished by conditions which people normally consider "unhappy". Illness and injury as such involve neither happiness nor unhappiness. People's ideas and attitudes toward life are what allow illness and injury to make them miserable.

December 22, 1974

Winter sunshine coming through the window fell on the petals of cyclamen, forming delicate shadows among the blooms. The beds had been pushed aside into the corners of the room and were covered with snow-white sheets. I entered it in my new wheelchair. As usual, I had on my bathrobe with only one arm through a sleeve (the joints of my elbows and shoulders had become so stiff that I could not wear it with both arms in the sleeves). This was the room that the chief nurse had arranged to let us use for my baptism because I was not able to travel to the church for the ceremony.

"Congratulations!" Members of the church greeted me cheerfully as they arrived for the occasion.

Reverend Funaki prayed, everybody sang a hymn, then I professed my faith:

"I believe in God the Father, Jesus Christ, and the Holy Spirit." The minister moistened my forehead with three drops of water and prayed that I lead a life based securely in my faith until the time came for me to return to our eternal home in heaven, and that I would follow the word of God and be supported by His love. Again we sang a hymn.

Among the people singing was Miss Annaka. Mr. Kamata, who had decided to go to seminary, was also there. Every week for a year he had come to sit by my bed, read the Bible, pray, and talk with me. Miss Watanabe was standing a little way back. For the past two years she had come to help with my meals and other daily chores. She had been a tremendous help to my mother and me. She did not talk much about the Bible, but her eyes always seemed to reflect her deeply-felt prayers.

Although I understood only a small part of the Bible on a very shallow level, I wished to obediently follow God's command: "Come to me." I did not expect my baptism to relieve my physical anguish, but I wanted to kneel before God who would patiently pardon the ugliness inside of me made up of envy, hatred, and intolerance. I knew I would continue to commit the sins proscribed in the Bible no matter how many times I was forgiven. There would be days when I would scream with pain. Yet I had decided to live my life following the blameless one who said on the cross:

"Forgive them, Father! They don't know what they are doing."

After the ceremony, I talked a while with the gathered group. Having been confined to a small hospital room for so long, I was nervous talking with such a large number of people, but haltingly I spoke to them about my mother.

I said that I had lost many things because of my injury, but it seemed that I had been given more than I had lost. Before I was hospitalized, my mother had not been a very attractive figure to me. During the day she had crawled on all fours, digging up our field, and at night she had done her piecework under a dim light, complaining about our lack of money. She had fainted when she heard about my accident. Her legs failed her when she saw my throat after the first tracheotomy. If my mother had been "strong" in the conventional sense of the word, she may have thought of some way *not* to sacrifice herself for me. She may have figured out how to go back home to her own life. But she had a weakness which made her incapable of leaving me alone in the hospital. This very weakness may have been the strength that supported my mother.

Had I not had the accident, I would not have seen her as she really is, a mother full of love. I may have spent my life a miserable person arrogant enough to regard his own mother as no more than a peasant woman covered with dirt.

> Pale flowers have
> The colors of Mother
> Mingled with weakness and sadness
> Their colors possess
> The warmth of Mother

> (Roses)

CHAPTER SIX

Welcoming Tomorrow

March 1975 to October 1978

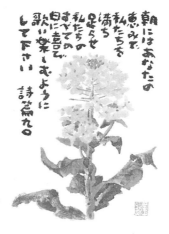

(Rape blossom)

From the Doctor's Report

No special therapy is prescribed. I talked to his mother about institutions where he could be sent for rehabilitation, but there are none capable of looking after him twenty-four hours a day. That there is nothing more modern medicine can do for him makes me feel all too painfully my limitations as a doctor. We can do no more than wait for him to find a means of leading his own life.

From Mother's Reminiscences

Thanks to the special-order wheelchair, we began taking walks around the hospital and were even given permission to go home for a visit. But as we became more and more comfortable, staying in the hospital seemed less and less justifiable. We talked about whether to go home or to admit Tomihiro into an institution. Going home would be best, but being so far out in the country away from the doctor was just too much of a worry. Tomihiro still broke out in fevers, and the danger of the slightest change leading to death had hardly decreased at all since his early days in the hospital.

Someone recommended a hospital in Tokyo for severely handicapped people, so I had my oldest daughter go and see it. The facilities were excellent, she reported, but the staff could not be expected to do any more than the minimum required for daily life. For example, they probably would not be able to help Tomihiro draw his pictures. The paints have to be squeezed out onto the palette, and the colors mixed according to his direction. After each stroke the brush has to be dipped in water or paint, and then put back in his mouth. Then the paper has to be held in front of his face. After he has drawn a stroke or two, the brush has to be.... I could never ask a member of the hospital staff to do something that took so much patience. So entrusting him to an institution also seemed unlikely. Still, we could not stay indefinitely in the hospital. Where could we go?

January 15, 1975

Two girls, all dressed up in kimonos, came into my room. I had forgotten that it was Adults Day. The two girls must have turned twenty during the last year, and just come from the ceremony honoring them and other twenty-year-olds as new adults. I thought they might be the twin daughters of one of the other patients in the room, but they came over to my bed. They nudged each other and began giggling.

"Hi, Sensei," they said as they made a little bow to me.

"Hmmn? Oh...wow! I thought I'd seen those two mugs before; it's you two!"

These two kimono-clad young ladies were Deme and Kimi. They had been members of the gymnastics club at Kuragano Junior High at the time I injured myself. All through junior high school and even after they had gone on to high school, they had continued to call me *sensei* and come to visit me sometimes. Deme had become a beautician, and Kimi was a saleswoman in a store. They were now both responsible, working members of society; but when they were with me, they turned back into unsophisticated young girls. We always enjoyed laughing and joking together.

When had the two become old enough to celebrate Adults Day? After the coming-of-age ceremony, they had taken a taxi from Takasaki and arrived at the hospital out of breath, their fancy hair ornaments swinging from their Japanese-style coiffeurs.

"Congratulations. You two half-pints have really become fine adults."

"That's right. Even we can become adults, but, I'm afraid, only on the outside."

The *obi* sashes tied around their middles looked uncomfortably tight, but they managed to laugh as uncontrollably as ever.

"Are they your classmates, Hoshino?" the man across from me asked after they had left. He had seen the dressed-up girls reflected in the mirror.

I thought back to those two precious months at Kuragano Junior High. I had managed to stretch four years of college into five and spent the winter of my final year on ski patrol duty at Nozawa Hot Springs. I had started work in December and finished up on March 30. That left me a week before my teaching job began.

April 8 was the first day of the school year. My face was snow-tanned so dark that you could hardly tell it from the back of my head. When I got up on the stage in the assembly hall to introduce myself as a new teacher, even my black face flushed, and my tongue got all tangled up.

"My name is Homihiro Hohino," is what came out.

Even though I had been enrolled in the school of education, I had graduated without acquiring any interest at all in teaching. I managed to get a job, but I was at a loss when I was informed that I would be teaching the seventh through ninth grades. I had no idea what I should do. I did everything I could, however, to act so that the kids would not figure that out.

When the boys, with their identical, closely-cropped heads, were dressed in their P.E. uniforms, I could not tell one from another. I am not very tall, so I completely disappeared when surrounded by the ninth graders.

The girls were always shy. Whenever I passed them in the corridor, I could feel their eyes on me even from behind. Each day was a new adventure.

One morning as I came through the school gate, dozens of faces were watching me from the second floor. A girl nicknamed "Mouse" flew out from behind something and suddenly asked me,

"Sensei, which singer do you like?"

"Let me see. I like Tomoko Ogawa."

"Really? What's so good about Tomoko Ogawa?"

"That song, 'The Little Finger You Bit Almost Came Off,' sends shivers down my back."

[Note: This is a joke. The real title is "The Little Finger You Bit Hurts" and has more subtle implications.]

"What're you talking about? Yukari Ito sang that one!"

The next day Mouse came flying out from the same spot, unfolded a poster of some actress or other in front of my face, and ran off again. Thinking back, Deme and Kimi, with their mischievous smiles, were somewhere in the vicinity that day.

Once, while I was standing in the schoolyard, a ninth-grade boy on the second floor called down to me in a loud voice.

"Hoshino-*sensei*, is it true you graduated from Gunma University?"

"That's right!"

"If you major in phys ed, does that mean you don't have to do anything else?"

"No, you have to study other things, too."

"Looking at you, nobody'd ever think that! Anyway, I want to be a P.E. teacher, too. Think I'd make it?"

"I managed to, and it's not a bad business. You can do it!"

I wondered what that boy was doing now.

After school, when club was over and the students had gone home, I often stripped to the waist and ran around the school grounds. I would be tired out from teaching, but I wanted to run. The setting sun had a gentle, hazy effect on the schoolyard, and the early summer breeze felt good on my sweaty, bare chest.

"Hoshino-*sense-e-e!*" One day while I was running, I heard a high-pitched voice calling from some distance away. I climbed up on an old, broken cement-block wall and looked out over a field of mulberry trees. One noticeably-large mulberry tree was swaying back and forth.

"Here I am! Here I am!" called a voice from inside the branches.

"Whoever you are, what are you doing up there?" I

shouted.

"It's me, Izumi! I'm eating mulberries."

Sure enough, I could see arms and legs among the branches. Then Izumi's face peeked out from the leaves. Everybody called him "Izumi-*chan*," a nickname usually reserved for younger children, because he was the smallest of the seventh-graders. When I saw him in the front row at the school's entrance ceremony, I had thought he must have come to the junior high instead of the elementary school by mistake. I wondered now if Izumi had grown any taller.

I had only taught for two months, not long enough to have any bad memories. Without any effort at recollection, the beautiful scenes replayed themselves before my eyes.

I had many more memories of Kuragano Junior High. I remembered that along the road in front of the school was a long fence covered with silly graffiti. Someone had drawn something that vaguely resembled a human being. Right at its crotch there was a hole in the wall. Through that hole I could see a bent sycamore tree, and beyond that were the school grounds where P.E. classes were under way. I could hear whistles being blown in short bursts. The window of the wooden school buildings were open, releasing the voices of the student chorus.

I walked by the school in my memories. As far as I walked, the fence with its hole, and the school, remained in my vision.

March 1975

> With my very first box of crayons
> I scribbled tulips
> All over the walls and shutters
>
> Now I hold a felt-tipped pen in my mouth
> And find .
> I'm still drawing tulips

Once, when I was in the third grade, a picture of mine won a prize in an exhibit. Actually, it was not my picture, but I had been applauded and had received a certificate and a prize.

During art class I was trying to reproduce a picture of a giraffe in a zoo, a picture I had seen in a book. My teacher said,

"That picture is good. Paint it neatly and I'll have it put in the village art show."

I decided to do my best, and carefully painted each spot on the giraffe's coat. When I was finished, I proudly showed it to my teacher, who put her head between her hands and said,

"What on earth have you done?"

For a while I was not sure why my teacher was so disappointed, but it finally dawned on me. As far as I was concerned, lots of bright colors made for a good picture, and I had painstakingly done the giraffe's spots in red and

144

green, not to mention blue, pink, and a whole array of other colors.

I had never seen a real giraffe. My picture was rejected, and I was given another picture to paint for homework. So I sat on the porch at home and painted the autumn mountains. None the wiser from my first experience, I proceeded to paint the mountains as I had done the giraffe. My cousin, who was sitting nearby watching me, grabbed the pastels out of my hand and finished my picture of the mountains in a rough manner. I was upset about what he had done, but I took the picture to school the next day. My teacher put it in the art show, and I won a box of soap as a prize. Ever since then, all my friends and family have thought me something of an artist.

As time passed and the guilt wore off, even I began to think I could draw well, and I began looking forward eagerly to school art class. Of course I never won another prize. Indeed, none of my pictures was even entered in a show again. What remained, however, was my love of drawing.

My art was always limited, though, to drawing likenesses of my classmates and teachers or the scenery from my classroom windows on the back of notebooks during class. Occasionally I did water-color paintings of my beloved mountains in sketchbooks, but I never seriously took up drawing.

I tried to answer all the letters I received in the hospital, and I had begun to add pictures of flowers to my replies. My friends seemed to appreciate these illustrations, and this encouraged me all the more. Until then I had never really looked at flowers; but in the hospital, the flowers my friends brought were the only bits of nature I came in close contact with. Day after day as I lay gazing at the little flowers on the stand next to my bed or on the window sill, I was constantly amazed at the beauty of their shape and color. As a whole, I came to realize, flowers had no surplus parts nor did they lack anything. The flower was attached at just the right spot, and the leaves were equally well placed. The thickness of the stem was just right to balance the leaves and flowers. The leaves set off the color of the petals, and the flowers bloomed without undermining the color or shape of the leaves. A small branch of flowers always looked to me like a vast natural landscape.

> Just as one flower has fulfilled its purpose
>   and prepares to fall
> The bud next to it is about to bloom
> This one camellia branch
> Is a miniature of all nature

(Camellia)

I did not know anything about drawing, but I thought that if I could copy nature just as it was I should have a decent picture. I knew nothing about composition or how to use colors, but if God had made these flowers, they would bloom naturally in a perfect harmony of shape and color. With this in mind, the flower I was looking at would begin to look bigger and bigger to me. As I grew more immersed in drawing it, I would find myself feeling as though I had become as small as an ant and was crawling around the petals. I even imagined myself covered with yellow pollen.

To me, flowers were not merely beautiful, they also had a power that would sometimes strike out at me.

> Some are intertwined
> Some are craving toward heaven
> > or dangling in despair
>
> Flower petals are the ocean waves
> That strike the cliffs
> With the strength of waves as powerful
> As the distance they retrace their steps
>
> > (Chrysanthemum)

At night after the lights were turned out, when the solitary, dim light from the emergency exit lit up a flower in bloom, I would lie watching it, and the form of a person living in sorrow would blend together with that of a beautiful flower.

Flocked together in full bloom
You look so happy
But each solitary flower wears
A lonely expression

You're just like us humans

(Orchid)

You pressed my fingers around an azalea
Then you put one between the laces of the shoe
    on your artificial leg
You didn't say so, but you meant
    Let's not give up!

How're you doing?
That same red flower is back in bloom

(Azalea)

"I cried so much then that I exhausted my supply of tears. I should have saved some." Miss Ogiwara, who had cried so often at night, was discharged after a satisfactory recovery from her operation. She was able to go back to work, but she still came by to see me. Having a leg amputated, especially for a young woman, must have caused considerable agony; but, on her frequent visits to my room, Miss Ogiwara's face was a picture of joy.

Then she was admitted to a hospital in Takasaki. Three

years had passed since her first illness, but doctors feared she had had a recurrence.

I took my felt-tipped pen to write her a letter:

Hello, Miss Ogiwara. Today I'm sending you rape blossoms. This is the flower Miss Konno left by my window when she dropped by on her way to see you. So the whole time I was drawing it I thought, 'Miss Ogiwara, be strong! Hurry up and get better!' When I finished, I realized that the stem was too thick; but doesn't it look sturdy? Bees as big as a child's thumb with yellow stripes down their backs gather on these flowers. When my thumb was about that size, what I enjoyed most during rape-blossom season was catching those bees. I would tie a leash of cotton thread to one, and then fly it. The bees usually wouldn't sting, but once, just as I caught one, it got my hand.

Did it hurt? Well, from my experience of pain up to that point, it did quite enough to make me cry. The tears came out on their own, all I had to supply was the sound effects.

I remember that time amazingly well. I was by myself at the foot of a mountain in the middle of a field flooded with yellow flowers.

The sound of the wings of thousands of bees seemed to resound from the depths of the earth, and in the midst of it all a butterfly flitted about happily. I realized that even if I cried, there was no one to hear me. I suddenly felt lonely and ran to a distant field where my father was. My father looked at my swollen red thumb, glared towards the field I had just come from and exhibited appropriate anger.

'That rotten old bee! Next time I find him he'll get a good

piece of your daddy's mind.' As soon as I heard that, my loneliness and the pain in my thumb vanished, and I ran off to hunt more bees.

Miss Ogiwara was so pleased with this letter, she wrote in reply, that she could not bear to keep it to herself. She showed it to everyone who came to see her. Her letters gave me no idea of the seriousness of her illness, but the next year, when the southern winds brought the rape blossoms again, Miss Ogiwara left for heaven, leaving her beauty and radiance in my heart.

> In the wind blowing over the rape blossoms,
> I sometimes remember.
>
> In the shade of the azalea shrub
> You said you once fell backwards into,
>
> In the pictures by Gauguin
> We talked about together,
>
> I see reflections of you
> Who never grows old.

Because it was such a chore for my mother to hold my sketchbook without moving a muscle while I drew, I asked my brother to make a stand for me. I put lots of conditions on my order. I wanted a stand that could move easily from side to side and up and down, would absolutely not shake or jiggle, and could be folded up and stored in the corner of the room.

My brother miraculously managed to make a stand that met all these specifications, using steel pipe, springs, and parts of various machines. The time I could spend drawing was greatly increased. Also, with Mother's hands free, I could now use different colors. Within a border made using an oil-base felt-tipped pen, I painted a picture with water-color pens that a friend had recommended. I had never thought of them before as anything more than toys that children use to scribble with; but by mixing various colors, then dabbing at them with a moist brush, I could make amazingly beautiful variations.

I imitated the technique I had seen my junior-high teacher use. He would draw pictures with a fountain pen and then create a shade-effect by moistening the wet ink with his own saliva.

Come to think of it, that special teacher had taught me, beyond painting methods, all about the beauty of the mountains of my Azuma village.

In order to get the right effect for the soft colors of the flower petals, I discovered that, instead of drawing with the pen itself, it was better to apply it first to another piece of paper, pick up the color with a brush, and then use the thinned-down product on my picture. I also tried blunting the end of my brush to get a wider line. Each mistake taught me something new. The first picture that I drew with even the background colored in was of the first orchid I had ever seen.

> My immature pen
> Could never capture one-thousandth
> Of the beauty of this flower
> But I want to keep it in my heart
> Along with the affection of "N" who
>> Labored to raise it
>> Cut it
>> And brought it to me
> I want it to bloom forever within me
>
> (Orchid)

My first completed picture of an orchid, which I gave to Miss Watanabe

April 1975

> The people at the bed across from me
> Are quarreling in small voices
> Voices that seem squeezed out
> > from deep inside them
> > go on and on
> I bite down on my pen as if to crush it
> > and draw a camellia

(Camellia)

The quarrelsome persons were probably the children of the old man who lay motionless in the bed they surrounded. They were each griping about how difficult their situations were. Although they spoke in low voices, the room was too small to keep the rest of us from hearing everything. Those "children," all adults with families of their own, had been taking turns looking after their ailing father and were apparently worn out.

"I've got too much to do with just the kids."

"You-know-who doesn't spend very much time here."

"Why do I have to do so much? It's not fair!"

Their voices grew louder and louder. The five other patients in the room and their attendants tried to keep their eyes on their newspapers or magazines, but we all understood the plight of the quarreling relatives. A desolate chill seemed to envelope each bed. Worse, this sort of scene was not at all unusual in a hospital room.

Nobody welcomed this atmosphere, and when we recognized it, someone would always make a joke, and everyone would laugh obligingly in a desperate effort to avoid it.

I thought of my mother's hardship and of the loneliness of my father who woke up each day without my mother and then headed out for the field alone.

April 1976

I overheard an old man, who had been in the same room with me for a long time, as he talked with a visitor.

"See the guy over there? He can't move anything from the neck down. Something like that happens, and even a college education can't help you."

I had thought he was a nice man, but now I was seething in anger. After that, no matter how interesting a story he had to tell me, I screamed inside myself,

Old fool! I wish you'd croak!

At last the day that I had prayed and hoped for came when the "old fool" was released from the hospital. Supported on crutches, he came over to my bed and spoke to me in a quivering voice.

"Hoshino, don't give up. You've got to get better!" And then tears came rolling down his cheeks! I had gotten angry over such a trivial statement. I was ashamed of my narrow-mindedness.

My friend pushed my wheelchair outside
   under a cherry tree
And bent down a branch in full bloom
   burying my face in blossoms

Filled with irresistible joy
   I began
Munching on the flowers
   blooming closest to my mouth

Several mangy-looking dogs, who must have been equally happy over the flowers, came over to the tree and sprawled out underneath it.

"Lying peacefully under the flowers as they fall would be a wonderful way to die," said an older nurse's aid as she looked at the flowers. I understood how she felt. I was sure she had endured many hardships throughout her life. Cherry blossoms stay on the tree no longer than four or five days before they fall to the ground. Looking at them, one could feel the quiet force of the sadness which lies behind the joy in life.

No matter what the emotions of the person viewing them, they could not change the color of the flowers, nor postpone their falling one second. It didn't matter whether one viewed them with sad eyes or in the merry company of a "flower-watching" party. Even if a person hung himself from the tree, the flowers would continue to bloom right next to the dangling body.

If I spent my life mourning the fact that I would never be able to move again, would there be any change in the seasons as they come and go? If not, then was it not foolish to be sad in the midst of all these works of God?

> A person who can move
>> must have patience
>> to remain still
> But does someone like me who cannot move
>> need patience?
> When I realized this I could feel
>> the thorny rope called "patience"
>> which so tightly bound me
>> disintegrate

The first picture I did with paints was of a red azalea. I sent the picture along with a letter to Miss Kumagai, a student nurse who attended my church:

> I imagine that the biblical character Enoch wore glasses, was kind, and just a little plump. The resemblance leads me to a natural association of these three: Miss Kumagai, paints [*enogu* in Japanese], and Enoch.

Miss Kumagai gave me my first paints. That was the day my mother, the paints, and I began our battle. When I lay on my side with the sketchbook about eight inches from my face, I could barely see the flowers, placed on a nearby stand, that I hoped to reproduce. Other than that, there was nothing else in my range of vision. On the other side of the sketchbook, my mother would mix the colors as I asked for them. It always took an unbearably long time until I got the color I wanted. It was difficult to judge the amount of paint and water needed, and I never knew if the color was right until I actually put it to paper. As for my mother, she had not held a brush since her school days, many long years before.

"Just a little bit more blue...." My mother picked up the tube of black paint.

"Idiot! That's black!"

"Add some more water."

"Damn it! This is all wrong!"

This sort of one-sided exchange went on day after day. Some days ended without a dab of paint reaching paper. As time passed, however, my mother's ears began to distinguish between the meanings of the various ways I said "just a little more."

Unfinished orchid

I continued blaming her for all my mistakes and bad pictures, but somehow the number of flowers in my sketchbook increased, each a product of our combined efforts.

An azalea bloomed in the hospital garden
Looking as if she were about to rob a bank
My mother tiptoed out and broke off a branch
I showed my painting of it to the man in the next bed
     who said
"Now, that's a really nice lily"

(Azalea)

May 1976
The early-morning gloom of spring surged in
          trying to push down the *shoji* screens
The spring water made a lazy trickling sound
          as it spilled from the hollow bamboo
          into the stone pool
I slipped into *zoris* to go out
          and take a pee just beyond the garden
          where I could see a field of flowers dimly white

We were poor
Poor, but my birth in the mountain village
          gave me a glimmer of pride

"Would it be all right to go home for a visit?" I finally mustered enough courage to ask my doctor when he came by on his rounds.

It was spring and the cherry blossoms were out; the trees were beginning to bud, and it was getting warmer. The fresh greenery of Mt. Akagi, which I could see from the seventh floor of the new hospital building, had been beckoning me for the past few days. I had a burning desire to go home.

"Go home, eh? I think you're strong enough to do that."

I had been planning this request for a long time. It took me several days to get up enough courage to ask, so when I finally did, I was startled that the reply had come so quickly and easily. It was six years since I had last been home.

Two days later my brother drove in to pick us up. A one-way trip took an hour and a half, so just arriving in good shape was cause for concern. As the car left the Maebashi city limits, however, and sped past the neatly ordered rows of wheat and along the soft green of the mulberry fields, I gave a sigh and gradually relaxed.

The level of the Watarase River looked lower than I remembered, but I could hear the faint sound of the ever-flowing current. Japanese roses in bloom on the slopes along the road swayed in the wind of the passing car. There were groves of smoky-green trees with clusters of small red and blue roofs poking out among them. Here and there, huge cloth carp for Children's Day were still flying atop tall poles. The gold-colored pinwheels capping the poles clattered as they turned in the wind.

When we arrived, we found my father outside the house. He had spent hours in the garden waiting for us. I was lifted out of the car and laid on cushions on the porch where a soft breeze caressed my hot cheeks.

The sound of rushing water in the irrigation canal beside the house and the sound of rustling bamboo leaves only deepened the pervasive quiet. My ears, so used to hearing the sounds of mechanical equipment twenty-four hours a day, now rang faintly, like the static of a broken radio.

The slats of the ceiling boards were black with soot. Brown sheets of newspaper poked out from between them, left over from the days when we raised silkworms. My nose was tickled by the smell of *tatami* mats which I had completely forgotten.

"Well now, what would you like to eat? Anything you like," said Mother as she carefully brought a brimming cup of water to my lips.

"Anything hot would be great. I want something that Dad usually eats."

I was not trying to be polite; ordinary things that my father always had would be nothing less than a feast to me.

A bright red azalea bloomed in the garden, and beyond that the mountains surrounding my home soared serenely towards the sky. The spring greenery had climbed halfway up the mountains, welling up like a layer of silver foam to cover them. These mountains that I had grown tired of looking at as a child were now as beautiful as if I were seeing them for the first time.

Even after I returned to the hospital I could not forget their beauty. They taught me the importance of looking anew at things I was prone to take for granted because of my long stay in the hospital.

> For three days
> The tulips set by my pillow had been opening
>   and closing.
> They all looked the same, just ordinary tulips.
> On the fourth morning when I glanced at them
>   an almost unearthly color met my eyes,
> A color made by the morning sun piercing
>   the petals.
> The tulips, of course, had displayed that same color
>   right there, every morning.
> But in vain—my eyes and my mind had labeled
>   the flowers "ordinary."
>
> That morning I learned that in ordinary things
>   lies an unfathomable depth of beauty.

(Tulip)

I was now able to go home four times a year. Once, my sister who lives in Kamakura arranged her visit so that we could be home together. She said to her two children,

"Show your Uncle Tomihiro your gymnastics."
The two looked at each other sheepishly.

"Do what you learned at your gymnastics class. See, Nobu and Kazu have begun taking lessons. Knowing them, I'm not sure how much of the real thing they can do, but I hear the teacher makes them work."

The two children got down on the *tatami* mats and, concentrating carefully, did forward, backward, and side rolls over and over again. Every time they finished one, they stood up and raised both arms in an authentic finishing pose. Their awkward little figures were too cute for words. My sister spoke intently about how uncoordinated her children were, but what came across strongly to me was the kindness of my sister and her husband. Nobody had been more upset by my accident than my parents and my elder sisters. They must have been terrified by this sport which had completely incapacitated their brother. Despite this, my sister was letting her own children learn gymnastics. She knew. She knew how much I, whose job it was to teach the fun and benefit of gymnastics, had agonized over the nature of my accident and the fact that my students had seen it happen. She also knew how I still loved gymnastics more than any other sport. I looked up at her gentle profile, and I could sense that these were the reasons she was having her own precious children take it up.

"Don't worry, Tomihiro," my sister's smile seemed to say to me, "The kids are having a good time."

The car headed towards the sunset. Myogi, Asama, and Chichibu mountains stood out in bold relief, waiting out the rays of the evening sun. The vague shapes of buildings in downtown Maebashi stood arranged like tombstones.

How many times had I been home to visit now? At first I had felt relieved at coming back to Maebashi, but recently I was vaguely reluctant. Despite my immobility, I had become quite healthy. It was probably my growing feeling that I could manage outside the hospital that was making me resist returning to it.

Mondays, Wednesdays, and Fridays were surgery days at the orthopedics ward. On busy days four or five people would undergo operations—each bearing his own pain, battling his illness with one eye on his date of release.

The moment a patient left the hospital another took his place. The doctors and nurses were always hurrying about.

Had the number of patients really increased as much as I imagined? It seemed as though the pace of the hospital, and the rate at which patients came and went, had quickened since the time I first arrived.

In the midst of all this I was the only one who, not

receiving any particular treatment, was doing nothing more than drawing pictures and taking walks. The doctors never suggested that I go home for good or transfer to another hospital, but I knew that I had become healthy enough to leave Gundai Hospital. And my own wishes and needs were not the only concern; I had to start thinking of my mother.

How many years had Mother slept in the tiny space between my bed and the window, doing the work of my arms and legs? As soon as she became friends with another attending relative, the patient he or she was caring for would be discharged, leaving my mother alone to start the whole friendship process with the next "resident." How many times had she had to do this? She could never sleep easily on nights when someone in my room had had an operation. The tension made her shoulders stiff, she said. She would massage her left shoulder with her right hand, and then her right shoulder with her left hand. The more I pondered how Mother had given up her own life to take care of me, the more I felt the necessity to make some decision.

> If God would move these arms just once
> I'd be given the honor of massaging
>   my mother's shoulders
> Watching the pods of the humble shepherd's-purse
>   swaying in the wind
> I get the feeling that day may really come
>
> (Shepherd's-purse)

But I did not know what decision I could make. Even if I transferred to another hospital, I would probably need someone to stay with me. A smaller hospital would have fewer nurses, and Mother would have to work even harder than she did now. Moreover, there was no guarantee another institution would even accept me.

I was restless in the hospital, but I came in contact with all sorts of people. Even if indirectly, I had a glimpse of the outside world. I wanted most of all to go back to my home surrounded by the beautiful mountains, but I could not bear the thought of having no visitors and nothing to do. I would probably spend the rest of my life watching television.

While I brooded, the car moved on at a heartless speed. Wanting to delay my return to the hospital, I had my brother make a detour through Shikishima Park in the northern part of the city.

The Sunday-evening sun setting over the park was a delicate orange color. There were parents and children in sweat suits, and kids carrying bats on their uniformed shoulders. The shadow of our car, with Mother and me inside, slowed down among the long, slender shadows of people walking happily through the park toward the lights of their own homes.

CHAPTER SEVEN

Beginning A New Journey

April 1978 to September 1979

(Red flower)

From the Doctor's Report

No special notes to make. (Recently progress in wheelchairs has been made. We consulted a manufacturer and were finally able to have one made to order that he can operate with his chin. We took him to an exhibit of pictures painted by mouth by a handicapped man, hoping to give him incentive to continue his own work.)

April 1978

The beds in the large rooms were always full. I wanted
to view my pictures from a distance, but in my own room
they would quickly become the focus of everyone's
attention, so I did not want to do it there. I wanted to hide
my pictures from the eyes of others simply because I had
never studied drawing formally. It took such a long time
to do one picture that when I thought I had done a good
job I could barely contain my joy or my desire to show it
to others. Even so, I was reluctant. The harder I worked
on a piece, the more difficult it was to show it to others.

On a noisy Sunday afternoon in the hospital, the second
floor hallway leading to the outpatient clinic was the only
quiet, isolated place where my mother and I could go.
Large windows lined both sides of the hallway, letting the
sunshine in. Even in the winter it was as warm and bright
as a greenhouse. After my afternoon temperature check,
we took a radio-cassette player to that hallway. There we
could enjoy tapes of music and recordings of church
services turned up as loudly as we liked. We listened to
Bach's orchestral suites, Handel's *Messiah*, Vivaldi
concertos by I Musici, and hymn collections. Schubert's
Winter Journey was perfect for snowy days, and my
mother always enjoyed hearing the popular "Koga
Melodies." There were times when, basking in the warm
spring sun and gazing at the new cellophane-like leaves
on the ginkgo trees, my mother and I would doze off

peacefully.

This spot was also the site of my small art exhibits. When I had painted several pictures, Mother would arrange them up against the backs of the wallside benches and then, as soft music played in the background, I, the great artist, would be taken in my wheelchair through the impromptu gallery to admire my floral masterpieces (!). I could then at last tell whether the pictures, which I had painted so closely to my face, had been drawn off-balance or if the colors were out of harmony. The mistakes, including those I had tried to gloss over, always stood out like sore thumbs. On the other hand, the flowers to whom I had assumed a humble attitude and which I had drawn with my deepest concentration seemed to bloom on the canvas as in nature.

"That background color is strange."

"That chrysanthemum shows the time put into it."

"I told you not to use that color!"

Mother had become a competent critic.

At the sound of approaching footsteps, our exhibit would be closed temporarily.

"Mom, someone's coming!" Mother would hurriedly gather up all the pictures. Sometimes the security guard or a visitor who had lost his way would come by. As soon as they had passed, our gallery would be reopened. Then, until the night-shift nurses began their busy comings and goings, the dogs being used in experiments took up their mournful howling, and the evening sun glowed pink on

the ginkgo trees, my mother and I—just the two of us—
continued our private showing.

Mother and I watched as the evening sun
Slowly set in the tops of the ginkgo trees

Always by the same bench, we could watch
The sun linger a little longer each day
As if to assure us
Happiness was tiptoeing closer

Back in my room
Who had come?
Leaving a sprig of sweet smelling daphne in my vase

July 1978

I was cooling off in the shade of a cherry tree in the back
garden when someone called my name. Dr. Nishimura
and Dr. Koizumi from orthopedics were on their way to
the Center for the Handicapped to see an exhibit by Mr.
Washizuka; they wanted to know if I would like to go
along.

A victim of polio, Mr. Washizuka was severely disabled,
and he did oil paintings with a brush held in his mouth.
His exhibit had been written up in the paper, and I had
wanted to go. In order to go out, however, I had to get
official permission and arrange for a car to take me there,

so I had just about given up on the idea when the doctors
came along.

I rode in Dr. Koizumi's car to the Center and transferred
to my wheelchair on arrival. In the entrance hall was a
large painting which immediately caught my eye. I was
astonished to find out that it had been painted by Mr.
Washizuka with a brush in his mouth. I was struck by the
excellence of the picture and, at the same time, by my own
lack of imagination. My pictures were amateurish and
much too small to even be put in a category with real
paintings. More than that, I was ashamed to have judged
Mr. Washizuka's work using my own as a standard.

The director of the center, Minoru Kubota, a man with a
long, thin face, gave us a guided tour of the exhibit.

"Mr. Hoshino also draws with a brush in his mouth,"
Dr. Nishimura told Mr. Kubota. My face flushed with
embarrassment. Mr. Washizuka had painted more than
thirty pieces, all of them large in size. I studied each from
top to bottom, but none gave any hint of his handicap. I
would be in a tough position if Mr. Kubota thought mine
were as good as his. Still, I left the Center for the
Handicapped exhilarated by the possibilities of drawing
by mouth.

It was a hot summer afternoon.

February 1979

"Mr. Kubota wants to hold an exhibit of your work. I

think you ought to; what do you say?" Dr. Nishimura dropped by to see me.

"My pictures are too small, and not the sort of thing to be displayed where people can see them. Please tell Mr. Kubota that I shall be happy to show them when I can draw better and do some bigger pieces."

With this I closed the subject, not considering it worth further discussion. A month later, Dr. Koizumi dropped by.

"Look, you don't have to have a public exhibit, but at least let us show them to Mr. Kubota." So saying he left, taking my pictures with him. I was still uncomfortable, but I figured that if Mr. Kubota had a good look at them he would realize that they were not worth putting on display, and that would take care of the matter quickly. So I did not object further, but I felt a little bit sorry for the two doctors who must have given an exaggerated account of my abilities.

If only I had more talent...I felt a twinge of regret.

It was the end of March, time to put my potted primrose outdoors. I had just returned from a visit home when someone came to see me. I had almost forgotten his face, but it was Mr. Kubota from the Center for the Handicapped, who had wanted to exhibit my pictures. He liked mountains, he told me, and even knew Mt. Kesamaru in Azuma village, where I was born.

When it came to mountains, nobody could shut me up.

And as always, when I got going, I went on and on about the unspoiled ridge ways of Kesamaru. Mr. Kubota agreed with everything I said. Yes, he said, it certainly was a splendid mountain. This so encouraged me that I was practically in raptures, for here was a person who really knew all about one of my favorite places. At that point he said,

"By the way, I was really surprised by the pictures you lent me. Let's show them! They're wonderful."

This guy's technique is incredible, I thought.

"You mean, an exhibit?" I tried to turn him down a few times, but by now Mr. Kubota was in control.

"We're only talking about a display in the halls of the Center for the Handicapped, so it won't be a big deal. We just want to show them to trainees and people who are coming to the Center for therapy. Of course, even though it'll be small, we'll do our best to make it a good show."

"...I...I would be so embarrassed. It would be such an injustice to real artists!"

I said this half to Mr. Kubota and half to my mother, hoping that she would come to my assistance. Mr. Kubota next directed his attention toward her.

"I've been involved in social work for many years now, but one thing keeps coming back to me. Recently people are taking a greater interest in social welfare, which is good, but there's something important behind it that's been lost. No matter how much money people give to build better and better facilities, if the donor hasn't put his heart into it, it can't be called 'social work.'

"Too many people spend lots of money to put old people and handicapped children into institutions, and then don't go visit them.

"We have plenty of fine rehabilitation facilities, but society refuses to accept the people who come out of them. And now, here you are, a mother who has spent nine years being the arms and legs of her son. I want to present this loving relationship through the pictures painted by the brush of that son dipped in paint prepared by that mother."

Mr. Kubota's talk reminded me of the words in Paul's letter to the Corinthians written almost two thousand years ago.

> I may give away everything I have, and even give up my body to be burned— but if I have not love, it does me no good.

I finally gave my consent, but I could not get to sleep that night. How would they display such little pictures?

The next day, when we told the doctors and nurses about the exhibit, they were overjoyed. My mother and I were left to mope alone.

I had thought I would only show the pictures that I felt were done well. The theme of the exhibit, however, gradually began to change from that of pictures drawn with a mouth-held brush to an introduction of one person's life. It was decided that the first writing I had done with a felt-tipped pen and even pictures that were incomplete or badly done would be put on display.

I had all my sketchbooks taken out from the back of the closet at home and brought to me. The poems by Jukichi Yagi, Sakutaro Hagiwara, and Hisako Tateuchi that I had copied even though the effort had caused me to break out in a fever; even my little picture of the cottonweed. Each painstakingly-drawn stroke held a memory for me. I counted all my sketchbooks and found that there were more than ten.

April 1979

It was three o'clock in the afternoon. Everybody's day has a three o'clock, but for me it was special because it was when I was taken out of bed to ride in my wheelchair. There was no hospital rule; we had merely got into the habit of going out after the afternoon temperature check. It was also the time when Mr. Kubota came to discuss the details of my exhibit.

He said, "What do you think, Hoshino? How about writing two or three lines about how you felt while drawing a picture, or some other thoughts you may have, and hanging it next to your pieces? Then people who come to see your work will understand it better."

I was all for it. I had been taught so much by just looking at flowers; each little blossom seemed to be an extension of the vastness of nature. I had released my anger on flowers. I had also felt within me emotions that were too overwhelming to bear. Flowers seemed to be like words of God spoken to a doubting heart.

> I lay face up
> Griping about
> One person after another
> Then, from the corner of my right eye
> I saw some peach blossoms
> Laughing

(Peach Blossoms)

I too had thought about accompanying my pictures with a few lines. I worried, however, because words affect people directly, and I did not want to write anything I would regret later. To make myself understood, simple, honest statements would be best. But my ugly thoughts in their raw form would certainly repulse the readers. Mr. Kubota seemed to be able to read my thoughts.

"Why don't you take this opportunity and write down everything?" he suggested.

The exhibit was set to be held from May 15 to July 3. How much could I write, in my slow style, in a month? Moreover, how much of my heart and mind could I put into words?

Something inside me
    is laughing at the misfortune of others
Another's happiness is bitter
If only he couldn't move, like me!
These feelings feed on my encumbered body
The ugliness inside me
    swells larger and larger
Even greater than the sorrow over my
motionless arms and legs is the grief I feel
    because, despite my own faults
    I cannot forgive others

Only when I see flowers
And face a sheet of white paper
Do I forget my grief

I began to write only to be faced anew with my own ugliness. I could not write the truth, so I tried to cover it up. I decided that it must take more courage to unveil one's entire self than it would to embark on any other adventure.

May 15, 1979

The opening day of my exhibition had arrived. I lay in bed, restless and upset, thinking how wonderful it would be if I could just disappear. What was meant to be a quiet and discreet showing had been turned into a grand event by the local newspaper. Even a television station had got involved.

The newspaper had labeled it in large headlines "A Testimony of Life" and "Mother and Son Exhibit." The scene of the inevitable disappointment of the people who would go and see it kept replaying itself before my eyes. What would I do about people who actually knew me? They could not possibly lie and say it was a great show. How would they be able to give me an honest opinion? I brooded in advance over the embarrassment they would suffer. Doctors and nurses greeted me while making their rounds.

"This is the big day! I'll stop off on my way home!" was the usual comment.

"Well, Mom, shall we go home for a while?" What would I do if a real artist came to see the pictures? Good or not, I had done my best; still, I worried about people who would criticize their line or composition. I could hardly get my lunch down.

Shortly after noon, a young woman appeared in my room.

"I've been to see your exhibit. I'm an art student at Gunma University."

An art student! I felt like a criminal caught at the scene of the crime.

"Oh help," I mumbled miserably. She, however, continued to look straight at me.

"It was good...wonderful. I realized how much harder I

must work at my own art...really, it's true...." Large tears flowed from her eyes.

May 20, 1979

It was the first Sunday after the opening of my exhibit. I was out in the hallway in my wheelchair when some of the women attending their sick relatives at the hospital came over to see me.

"We went to see your pictures, Mr. Hoshino. We all cried...not out of sympathy or anything like that, the tears just began to flow. Your mother did a good job, too. I wanted to buy one, but there were little circles on all of them."

One of the ladies seemed to be remembering the pictures; she kept dabbing at her eyes with her apron.

"Good grief! I didn't plan on making you folks cry! Now dry your eyes, and *please* explain what the 'little circles' are supposed to mean."

"What? Don't you know? A circle means a picture has been sold."

"They've *all* been *sold*?" I simply couldn't believe it. Come to think of it, though, other people had been by to see me on their way home from the exhibit and had said things like, "I was a few minutes too late," or "That one had a circle." I finally realized what they had been talking about.

Before the opening, Mr. Kubota had asked me, "What shall we do if someone wants a picture?"

"First of all, there won't be anyone," I said, "but if by some fluke there happens to be, please, give it to the poor soul. Anyone who would want one of my pictures would have to be a little strange, but to me he would be a rare treasure." I refused to give the matter much thought. Certainly there would not be more than a request or two.

"If they're all sold, does that mean even my first paintings—that miserable cottonweed, and the *keyaki* tree I did for color practice?"

I was flustered. If they were really good it might be different, but I could not bear the thought of those awful pictures changing hands. Once again, I felt myself a criminal and quickly called Mr. Yutaka Ishida.

Mr. Ishida ran a gallery and had heard about my exhibit from one of the doctors in orthopedics. He had done the display of my work and given me advice when I most needed it.

As usual he spoke calmly but with authority. "They bought those pictures because they were impressed. It's not as though you forced them on anybody, so be proud of yourself! Everyone's thrilled with the exhibit, and there's no need to worry. Everything is going well."

I breathed a deep sigh of relief and, at the same time, I felt something new springing up inside me.

Just as Mr. Ishida said, the exhibit was a great success.

In the hall of the Center for the Handicapped where the pictures were displayed, a notebook was available for people to record their impressions. Everyday Mr. Kubota made a copy of what had been written and brought it to me at the hospital. Even his gait as he entered my room showed how pleased he, too, was.

"It's incredible, Hoshino. The halls at the Center are full of people. Groups are coming in by the busload. I have to admit that I myself never dreamed it would be this big!"

I was taken to the Center several times, and it was just as Mr. Kubota reported. People came and went constantly. They stood in front of the pictures and read the accompanying sentences at such a close range that they almost bumped their noses on them. There were even people with handkerchiefs held up to their eyes.

"My pictures can't be worth all this. There must be a mistake," I thought. But when I moved a little closer I saw that those pictures were unmistakably mine; and the people standing in front of them had their eyes focused straight ahead.

> Dear Mr. Hoshino,
> The pieces you've drawn with all your strength and surrounded by your mother's warm love have filled me with joy and pleasure. Thank you so much. I had hoped to have one to decorate my home, so I'm sad to see them all reserved.
>
> Teruko Oka
> May 19

I too am handicapped. In each of your pictures I could feel your pain, sadness, and joy clearly expressed. I am paralyzed from the waist down, and I was revitalized by your exhibit.

Kuroda

Congratulations, Mr. Hoshino!
All sixty pictures are yours, but each has a different face. I especially liked the columbine, the sweet daphne, the iris, and the pussy willow. I don't know how long I'll live, but it's how deeply and deliberately we live our lives that's important.

(Anonymous)

A picture comes from the heart. If it doesn't, no matter how famous the artist is, no matter how superior his technique, and no matter how beautiful a piece, it will not inspire emotion. But I will be moved by a piece accomplished, however badly, with a person's whole strength and being. Today I realized this afresh. I discovered again how lazy most of us are; we must ask ourselves what we should do with our lives and carry it through. I also draw pictures—I believe that my art must always be my mother, my earth, my light and air. A piece need not be artistically excellent, but I always hope that it will touch something in the viewer's heart.

I wasn't amazed at your work because of the fact that you draw with a pen in your mouth; I was struck by your spiritual strength. Thank you very much.

Ko Sekiguchi, kiri-e artist

Japanese Iris; p.74 (1978)

Lily; p.110 (1979)

Many people took time to write their impressions of my exhibit. Among them was Mr. Kubota's son.

> I don't know much about my father's work. But I've never been more impressed than I am today by my father who associates with and can even be of help to a man as pure of heart as you. Keep at it!
>
> Kazuki Kubota

Students, as well as others whom I had met during my two short months at Kuragano Junior High, came to the Center.

> I've only met you once before when I brought some forms to you at the hospital. My first impression was that of a

refreshed young man just back from exercising. I thought how handsome you were. But I ran away, not being able to say half the things I had planned to, nor even to look at you—you were so thin. But today when I saw your pictures I was moved, gladdened, and relieved. I was also ashamed of myself thinking how you, not able to move, live each day much more intentionally than I. I'm sorry that I can't express myself any better than this. Please continue your efforts.

The clerk with bad handwriting
from Kuragano Elementary School

Dear Mr. Hoshino,
I'm thrilled by your wonderful pictures and poems. What an abundant life you must lead. You overcame your pain and now live in the grace of God, filled with His special joy. Thank you for all you have taught me. I'm going to ask more people from Kuragano to come. Give your mother my best wishes for health and a long life.

Yajima, Kuragano

My wife and friends saw your pictures and encouraged me to come, but I wasn't able to right away. Today I finally came and was struck by your work as well as Mr. Kubota's talk. My personality is somewhat odd in that I rarely cry or get emotional. In your poem, "Rape Blossoms," you wrote, "I'll become a strong stem," and I wondered just how hard you had to struggle inside yourself before you could write those words. Your mother's love surely sustained you through the fight. The reality of your life must be an encouragement to many people, for you show just how endless the possibilities for

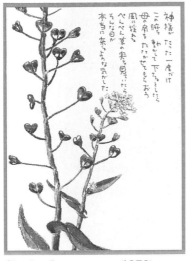

Shepherd's-purse; p.*163* (1979)　　　Rape Blossoms; p.*188* (1975)

human life are. It was this reality and your wonderful pictures (not even considering your handicap) that have touched me so deeply.

Please take care of yourself.

Koichi Nakajima

Impressions, encouragement, sympathy, personal stories, and familiar names of old friends filled up four notebooks. The pictures my mother and I had painted so surreptitiously in the hospital were no longer our private possessions.

The pictures had left me and my small room and set out on their own. They had stolen into the hearts of many different people and headed off on their own journeys.

The pictures that had taken the greatest toll in pain and endurance to create were the ones that traveled the farthest away.

As a matter of fact, I had had a similar experience several years before when "Mr. T," my friend and fellow sufferer, was discharged from the hospital, and I had given him a picture to remember me by.

> "T" used to take me for walks in my wheelchair.
> He was good at magic tricks and impersonations
> and never allowed the sound of laughter
> to die out in our room.
>
> The day he left the hospital,
> Mother and I saw him to the entrance.
> It was pouring rain, but as he left
> "T" turned back time after time to bow his head to us.
> I, too, lowered my head as far as I could.
> "T" waved to me from the car. I can't wave, so
> I stuck out my tongue and wagged it back and forth
>
> I watched him and my picture "Iris" go
> until they were out of sight

The sixty pictures I had painted over five years had all left me, but I was lighthearted.

"Even if you work hard to raise a daughter, someday you have to let her get married and leave home. Then you start wishing you had done this or that while she was still with you. It's the same with a painting; it's not until you let go of it that you finally understand it." I could identify with these words spoken to me by an associate of Mr. Ishida.

After the exhibit was over, Mr. Kubota continued to come and talk with me. He also advised me on a problem which I had brooded over for a long time: whether to go home or to an institution after leaving Gundai Hospital. Mr. Kubota gave his advice unhesitantly.

"If you're strong enough to live outside of a hospital, of course you should go home. No matter how good its facilities, an institution is an institution. If you have a home with people who will care for you, then that's where you belong. There's nothing warmer than the love of your family."

I felt the wisdom behind the words of this man who had been involved in social work for so long. I decided to follow his advice.

"That's it, we're going home." I felt a little uneasy about being so far from a hospital, but I no longer conjured up the vision of myself being cooped up, sad, and friendless in my home in a remote mountain village.

"You've got your drawing and your talent for writing. Go home and write. I plan on leaving my post at the end of this year, but I'll be rooting for you. I'll stick with you until the day I die."

I had met a really good man.... And, yes, part of me had already left the hospital. Were not my pictures and poems decorating living rooms and entryways in homes outside the hospital? Had not society given me a warm welcome back?

> A stem had broken
>> as easily as my neck
> It was there that
>> a bud appeared
>> and then a bloom
> I drink the same water as this rape blossom
>> and take in the same sunlight
> I'll become a strong stem

(Rape Blossoms)

September 14, 1979

The doctors had wracked their brains, exhausted their resources, and finally come up with an electric wheelchair for me. I could drive it with my chin, the only part of my body that I could move freely. I had driven it every single day since it was first delivered at the end of April. I could now move about as easily as if the wheels were my own legs. But on this day in September, I had suddenly lost my expertise and reeled about like a beginning driver.

My mother attended to my needs as surely and efficiently as the nurses who had taught her. The head nurse had already been in to see me three or four times that morning, taking her reluctant, but nonetheless cheerful, leave of me.

Watching the slim fingers of the nurse who took my pulse for the last time, I felt as if all my willful behavior, each selfish act I had committed during the past nine years, was now forgiven.

"Thank you, everyone, for your help and encouragement. I hope that all of you will get better and be able to leave the hospital as soon as possible. I'll be sure to visit when I come to the outpatient clinic." How many times had I heard these words? It had to be more than a hundred. Even I had said them many times. I had only done it as a joke, however, mimicking the familiar words to make people laugh when I left my room to go for a walk. (Once somebody in the room next door had overhead me and come running!)

But today, I realized I was saying these words in all seriousness, and I felt my eyes become suddenly hot. Nobody in my room laughed.

As Mother and I left, we found the attendants from other rooms waiting in the hallway to say good-bye to us. They grasped my mother's hands and cried with her.

I tried my best not to cry, but when it seemed the tears were going to fall, I began singing to myself in a small voice. I told myself not to cry. I couldn't wipe my own face, and if I asked my mother to, she would only start crying again. If some stranger saw me in the wheelchair with my cheeks wet, he would think I was crying tears of sadness.

The Gunma mulberry fields spread out along one side of the gently-sloping base of Mt. Akagi. Our car was homeward bound with the autumn sun on its back. It sped along the narrow road between the mulberry trees and past rows of small houses. I had grown used to this road having traveled it each time we had been back to visit, but this time each bit of scenery appeared as fresh as the first time I had seen it. I wondered if my heart was pounding because I had at last found the road home.

A village one might expect to find anywhere in the mountains of Japan, that was my home.

From the time I was small, my father had often told me, his eldest son,

"When you grow up, go work in the city. If you stay here, you'll end up having to spend the rest of your days crawling around in these fields that won't grow anything anyway."

My father was the eldest son in his family and thus in line to take over the family farm. In 1921, at the age of eighteen, he abandoned his responsibilities to run off by himself to Tokyo. To avoid being discovered by his parents, he had changed clothes in the mulberry field beside the house and taken only a single small bundle with him. He had confided in his younger brother who was the only one to see him off at the train station. After years of hardship, Father had finally achieved a measure of success. Then, on March 10, 1945, a few months before the end of World War II, all of his efforts were reduced to cinders in an air raid. My father's disappointment had been firmly instilled in me.

It may have been partly because of this influence that I had grown up planning my escape from that mountain village. This was also true of most of the other kids I grew up with. Even as a child, as I watched my parents stooping in the muddy, narrow fields, it was impossible to ignore the premonition of what my own future would be like if I stayed there. My parents had to sell their meager crops for low prices. During the winter they cut trees on the mountain, endangering their lives to bring them down on sleds.

When older boys in the neighborhood left for the city as adults, they would come back for New Year's or the Bon Festival wearing new suits and bearing sweets that would melt in your mouth. They, and the children they brought with them, wore clean clothes and spoke politely in a manner that carried a scent of the city. I actually believed that they lived in a place which held the power to turn everything into happiness.

I, too, left for the city. It was a wonderful place, bright and full of unusual things, lively and convenient. The city people had no idea that my father was back in the mountains chopping wood, nor did they know how dirty

my mother's hands got as she peeled persimmons and
hung them from the rafters to dry.

   While in college, I wrote poems like this one:

Next time I go home
I'll wear a dark suit
Shine my shoes so brightly I can see my face
And comb my hair neatly

With a big suitcase in each hand
I'll step smartly off the bus
As I walk along a path through the fields
A muddy face will pop up from among the ears of wheat
"You on vacation?"

Embarrassed but determined
I'll reply in the tones of townsfolk
"Not yet. Today is Sunday, you know."
The dogs will howl
Thinking me a big shot from the village office

   During the winter, these people who made their living
cultivating little fields and raising silkworms went up the
mountain every day to collect firewood. Now, that
certainly would not be categorized as mountain climbing.
   Mountain climbing—what a citified sport. I left my

village only to spend money I could not spare to exhaust myself climbing the Japanese Alps. Had I been looking for mountains different from those of my home? Some of the mountains I had climbed were not even as majestic as the one behind my house. Then I was driven to rock climbing—the pursuit of more severe and rugged slopes. But what I saw on the other side of those summits were the mountains of my home.

As my brother's car rounded the base of Mt. Akagi, we entered the familiar valley where the Watarase River flows. The Ashio Line—one of the biggest money-losers in the Japanese railway system—tooled leisurely along just below the highway overlooking the river whose white, granite-flecked bank was crossed by the afternoon shadow of the mountains. Old houses, as close as family touching shoulders, snuggled up against the mountains which had, over millions of years, been carved into the most comfortable form possible and were now quietly guarding the houses.

The reasons why I had first hated and left this place and then later missed it so badly were the same. I had grown tired of looking at the same scenery day after day and worked so hard to escape that I failed to see that it was what had made me what I am. All the roads I had taken to find something new had been leading me right back home.

Now I was heading back to those all-too-familiar

mountains, those hills of home as soft as my mother's lap. I had not been able to bring back even one of the happy dreams I had envisioned as a boy as I faced the mountains; but I was going home with new pride and appreciation.

To be sure, I had nothing tangible to show for myself. But in my heart I had the living knowledge born of my long suffering and experience of hopelessness that something invisible was sustaining all things visible.

The pale red ears of the eulalia blowing in the breeze peeked over the guardrail. Ahead of us, I could see our village, dyed red in the full autumn sun. I had left home and could now reclaim it; it was not until I had lost it that I realized its worth. I had been saved from agony by agony; I had dug a hole of sadness only to have joy spring out of it. I know now how interesting life is and how good it is to be alive!

There is much more to come, for I shall continue to write the words that only I can write, in the bosom of the mountain that holds out both arms to welcome me.

AFTERWORD

During my stay in the hospital, I used to gaze at the sunflowers blooming in the garden of the nursing school and think about how, if I were ever lucky enough to be released, I would like to grow sunflowers in my garden at home. This summer we have had a lot of rain, but there are now sunflowers blooming in the yard that are as big as wash basins.

When I go out for walks in my electric wheelchair, women from the neighborhood call out to me as they work in their terraced fields.

"I bet you're glad to be home. It's the best place to be, eh?"

Surrounding every house I pass are old trees that serve as wind breaks. When I was small, I climbed every one of them. The people from my hometown have welcomed me much more warmly than I had imagined.

I have to admit that it has not been easy writing about my stay in the hospital after finally managing to come back home. I know my mother, who helped me write it, feels the same way. There are so many things that I would like to forget. I cannot write quickly to start out with, but it took an especially long time when I had to write about painful experiences. In the end, I could only describe a small part of them. One of my greatest fears was that the sadness in my heart would be quickly linked with my physical disabilities and would not be understood as I meant it.

After completing this book, however, I feel refreshed. Since I came home, I have been contributing pictures and poems to the bi-monthly magazine *Some Day Somewhere*. One line I wrote was, "the dark of night is what makes the morning light so brilliant." This book took me seven months to write, and I am now enjoying the even-brighter light of morning.

Finally, I would like to thank the doctors and nurses of Gundai Hospital who have helped me get as well as I am, and Dr. Nishimura who wrote the doctor's reports for this book.

I also want to thank the members of Maebashi Christian Church who have supported me with their prayers, Mr. Minoru Kubota who advised me on all matters pertaining to the publication of this book, everyone else who has given me encouragement, and Mrs. Sonoko Yamazaki from Rippu-shobo who came to see me in Azuma so many times.

I feel that I am ready to take one more step away from "the depths."

Tomihiro Hoshino
Azuma Village
November 1980

TRANSLATORS' NOTES

When *Love From the Depths* was originally published in 1981, Mr. Hoshino was just emerging as a topic of conversation within Gunma, the prefecture where both Azuma and Maebashi are located. In the ensuing years, he has become a household word in this area and is now very well known in all parts of Japan. His pictures and poems have been exhibited throughout the country, his various books are available in any bookstore you might happen upon, and his calendars decorate homes everywhere. Three hundred thousand people a year make the trip to Azuma to visit the art museum built by the village as a permanent home for his works.

Mr. Hoshino's story is a unique one in that his insight and talents are eloquent in their simplicity. It has been widely read in Japan by not only Christians and people with handicaps, but also people from many other walks of life. Even the most unimpressible teenager finds Mr. Hoshino's casual style easy to understand and appreciate. People who are interested in Christianity but who still have plenty of skepticism relate willingly to his initial doubts about religious "hocus-pocus" and his embarrassment about being prayed over in front of a roomful of other patients. Adults who are overwhelmed by the drudgery and responsibility of working and raising families and older people who feel they have outlived their usefulness are given new encouragement that they are necessary and do have special talents and purposes that are just waiting to be discovered. In fact, the section where Mr. Hoshino discovers the passages in the Bible that describe the value of the "weaker parts of the body" and indicate the will of God for every living being on earth may be the most important part of the book. Readers with a Christian background have probably heard this message so many times that it has lost much of its impact, but for Mr. Hoshino the discovery proved to be a watershed experience. For him and many of his Japanese readers these words have provided an entirely new outlook on life.

From the perspective of a different culture, it may come as a surprise to read that Mr. Hoshino spent so many years in a hospital and that his mother was there with him the entire time. These aspects are very Japanese. In most hospitals you will find large numbers of long-term patients and family members, usually women, who attend to them on a full-time basis. The modernization of medical practices and smaller nuclear families, however, will probably see the demise of the attending mother, and we imagine that the next generation of Japanese readers will be as amazed as anyone else that Mrs. Hoshino dedicated such a long period of her life to the care of her son.

Love From the Depths will appeal to Western readers in much the same way it has to the Japanese, but it is also valuable for the way that it portrays the Japanese culture. The Japanese have been described for years as camera-wielding tourists who travel in packs. Of late, the main image is of ruthless businessmen buying up real estate at lightning speed. Having lived in Japan for a combined total of fifty-five years, we would like to say that the descriptions of people and attitudes given in *Love From the Depths* are the more accurate.

We would like to thank Mr. Hoshino for allowing us to translate *Love From the Depths*. It was a great pleasure to be able to work on such a wonderful book and doubly so because we were able to do it together. We would also like to thank Ms. Sonoko Yamazaki, Mr. Hoshino's editor at Rippu-shobo, and David Swain, distinguished translator and now-retired UMC missionary, who kindly read through our manuscript, liberally applied his red pen, and gave us much encouragement. We are also thankful to our families who have supported us in this project, from beginning to end.

Deborah Stuhr Iwabuchi
Kazuko Enda
Maebashi and Ebina
July 1994

About the Author

Tomihiro Hoshino was born on April 24, 1946. He attended schools in Azuma and graduated from Kiryu Boys' High School. He was then admitted to the School of Education of Gunma University. After graduation, he was employed as a teacher of physical education at Kuragano Junior High School in Takasaki. After only two months of teaching, he was injured in a fall during gymnastics practice. As a result, he was paralyzed from the neck down. He was hospitalized for nine years, and now lives at home, where he continues to paint and write poems using a brush held in his mouth.   Photo by Koei Iizima

About the Translators

Kazuko Enda grew up in Tokyo. She attended the University of the Pacific as part of her college career and graduated from Aoyama Gakuin University in 1979. She is a freelance translator and lives in Ebina with her husband Hitoshi and her son Yohei.

Deborah Stuhr Iwabuchi was raised in California and moved to Maebashi in 1978 after graduation from the University of the Pacific. She is a freelance translator and lives with her husband Ikuo, daughters Manna and Hikari, and mother-in-law Hideko.

Love From the Depths
—— ラブ フロム ザ デプス ——
英訳版 『愛 深き淵より』

著　者	星野　富弘
訳　者	岩淵デボラ＆遠田和子
発行者	鎌倉　　豊
発行所	立風書房 〒153 東京都目黒区上目黒5-5-8
	TEL03-5721-0561（営業）
編　集	山崎園子
印刷所	図書印刷株式会社